HOW ANYONE CAN FIX AND REV UP PCs

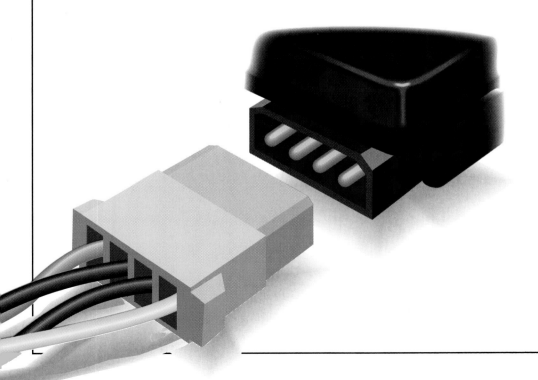

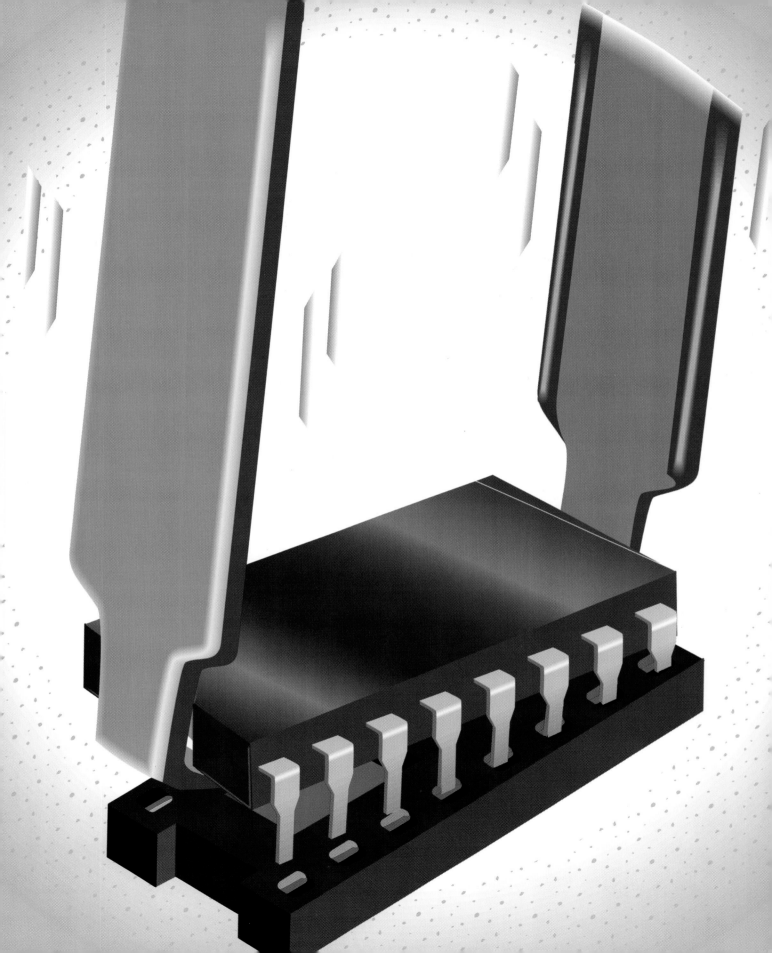

HOW ANYONE CAN FIX AND REV UP PCs

RON WHITE

Illustrated by
CARRIE ENGLISH

Ziff-Davis Press
Emeryville, California

Development Editor	Melinda Levine
Technical Reviewer	Sally Neuman
Illustrator	Carrie English
Project Coordinator	Ami Knox
Proofreader	Carol Burbo
Cover Illustration	Carrie English
Cover Design	Regan Honda
Book Design	Carrie English
Graphics Editor	Dan Brodnitz
Word Processing	Howard Blechman
Page Layout	M.D. Barrera and Bruce Lundquist
Indexer	Valerie Robbins

Ziff-Davis Press books are produced on a Macintosh computer system with the following applications: FrameMaker®, Microsoft® Word, QuarkXPress®, Adobe Illustrator®, Adobe Photoshop®, Adobe Streamline™, MacLink®*Plus*, Aldus® FreeHand™, Collage Plus™.

If you have comments or questions or would like to receive a free catalog, call or write:
Ziff-Davis Press
5903 Christie Avenue
Emeryville, CA 94608
1-800-688-0448

ISBN 1-56276-252-4

Manufactured in the United States of America
✪ This book is printed on paper that contains 50% total recycled fiber of which 20% is de-inked postconsumer fiber.
10 9 8 7 6 5 4 3 2

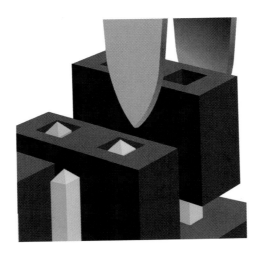

For L.V. White, my father,
who would have loved to
tinker with these things

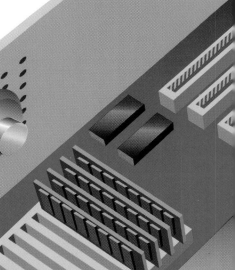

There is a little bit of a lot of people in this book. People from the IBM Compatible Users Group in San Antonio, people from *PC/Computing*, and people I've met but never seen on ZiffNet and CompuServe and on countless other local electronic bulletin boards. One of the great things about personal computing is that I've never met a computer user who wasn't willing to share his or her knowledge with others. In the early '80s when the personal computer revolution was booming, there weren't many sources of help, just a few books, *PC Magazine*, and user's groups. Without others to turn to when a screen went blank, a disk drive went *grunch,* or an entire system went south, many of us would have been in a fix.

So I must thank all those people, whom I'm not going to try to name because I'm sure I'd leave someone out. You know who you are. Exemplifying what is best in all these generous and good-hearted souls is one I must single out: Sally Neuman. Sally is the former sysop of *PC/Contact* on ZiffNet, the author of *PC/Computing*'s late "Q&A" column, and now a senior system operator for the Interchange database system. In those positions and as head of her own consulting company in Washington, she has been a continuous source of help for computer users literally from all over the world. She's the Florence Nightingale of computing, not simply because she is so willing to help others but also because her advice is always so uncannily accurate. Until I met Sally, I really didn't think the human brain was capable of holding so much information about computer hardware. But I was quick to recognize a good thing when I saw it, and was happy to get her as not only the technical editor of this book but as an advisor for many chapters before I started writing them. Thanks, Sally.

And I must thank Carrie English, the artist who turned my scribbled sketches and out-of-focus photos into genuine works of art. Her illustrations are crucial to this book because they say so much more than words can and make working with computers appear as simple as it really can be if you're not overwhelmed with the visual clutter that greets you when you first crack the case of a PC.

Melinda Levine, my editor at ZD Press, deserves special thanks for now having suffered through three books with me. Invariably, when I'd see her edits of my original text, I'd be embarrassed that I'd written such awkward words and happy that she'd rescued me. Thanks also to Cindy Hudson, publisher at ZD Press, for her support on all these books.

Les Mitchell gave me my first lesson in computer repair. At the time, I was working as an editor at a newspaper where Les was one of the people responsible for maintaining the pre-PC computerized editing system we used. One day, the display on my monitor began to look as if it had been filtered through a tornado. The text was skewed and stretched into a work of modern art. Of course, I called Les. He took one look at the monitor and slapped the top of it—hard. The monitor's text obediently snapped back into place.

I'm not advocating violence against PCs—as tempting as it may be at times. Les, of course, had a secret weapon—a storeroom full of replacement monitors in case slapping around my monitor didn't help or even made things worse. But it taught me two things. One is that many computer problems are only a matter of a couple of pieces of metal not making proper contact with each other. When Les slapped my monitor, he was jarring something inside back into place. The other—and more important—lesson was that I shouldn't be afraid of computer hardware—or, more properly, that I shouldn't be afraid of hurting it. Computer equipment will withstand a lot of abuse and endure a lot of misuse without complaining. As mysterious and powerful as computers may seem at times, at their heart they are simply machines that obey all the laws of physics as surely as a toaster or a lawn mower.

That's what I want to convey in this book: That a PC is simply another tool of modern times and that you shouldn't be any more afraid to work with it—or on it—than you would with any other tool. There are a lot of other books out about how to repair and upgrade PCs, but most I've seen make the task seem more daunting because they are filled with charts and tables and instructions most people will never use. I've tried to focus on the simple, but not always obvious, things that are common to most computer maintenance and repair. This advice is based on experience from the many years when I didn't work for a company with a support staff. I learned how to make the most common PC repairs and upgrades myself through trial and error. I'm hoping to spare you the errors. And I'm hoping to share with you the little secrets that never seem to make it to other repair and upgrade books—the little piece of metal you have to bend to make an expansion board slip in, what to do if you break off a tab that holds a memory SIMM, and most importantly, how to recover from a computer disaster that catches you after hours, when you can't turn to support staff, user group members, or friends for help. Fixing up PCs doesn't have to be a terror. It can even be fun.

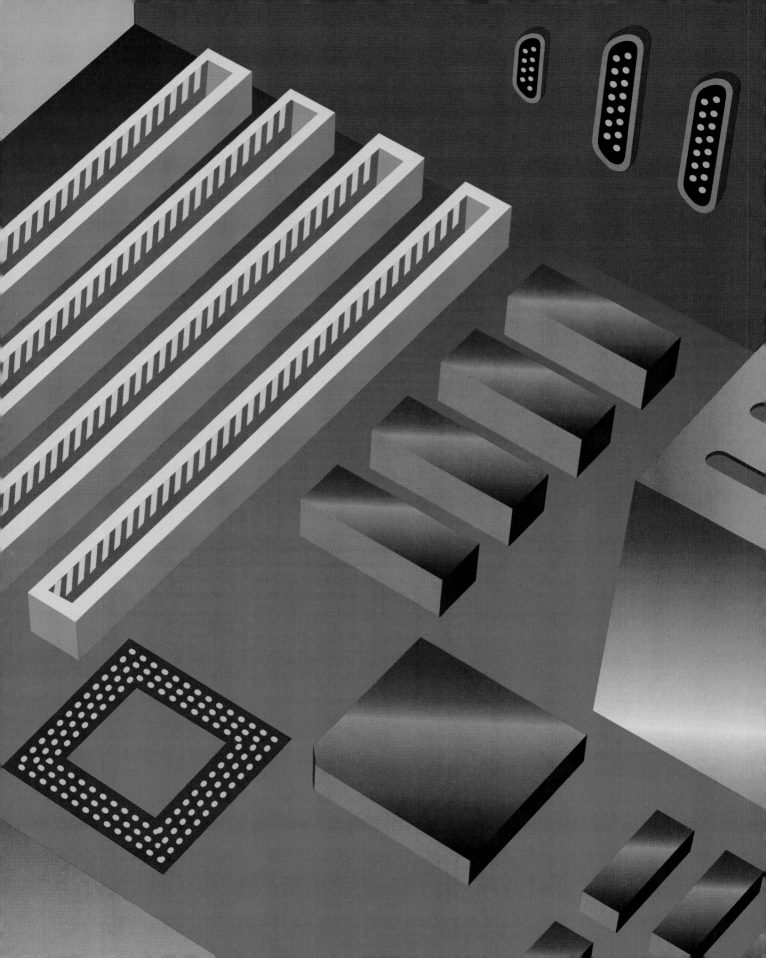

GETTING TO KNOW YOUR PC

CONTENTS

O V E R V I E W

THE SCARIEST THINGS are those that have no names—mysterious creatures that possess who-knows-what hidden dangers that may send us sprawling. Personal computers are one of those scary things. Many adults have never been taught what a microchip is, what a computer port does, or the name for that little metal sliding contraption on a 3½-inch floppy disk (a shutter). What we did learn was that computers are extremely expensive and fragile mechanisms, and that only the initiated—people in white lab coats sporting pocket protectors—were allowed to work on them. Opening a PC was as terrifying as opening the Ark of the Covenant. When you cracked the case on a computer, unless you were pure of heart and had the special wisdom known only by computer geeks, you were likely to get blown away like the Nazis in *Raiders of the Lost Ark.* Or, almost as bad, you might destroy that expensive electronic gadget that cost thousands of dollars.

But there is no reason to be afraid of hurting yourself or your computer. PCs are exceptionally durable machines—far less likely to be damaged by your tinkering than is the family car. They have few moving parts—the most likely components for wear and tear. And with one exception (discussed in Chapter 2), nothing you do from the keyboard will damage your computer. None of the software you would normally use does anything that would break your hardware. You can issue any sort of command at the DOS prompt and double-click on everything in sight in a Windows program, and you'll never *physically* harm your PC or its paraphernalia.

Notice I said *physically*. Although you can't use software to inflict physical damage on your computer, it is possible to *logically* damage the data and programs you've stored on your PC's drives. You can erase files that you didn't intend to erase and you can reformat or repartition a hard drive so that everything on it is deleted. But even in these situations, there are programs designed to help you recover from such disasters. The best known is the Norton Utilities, which has unerase and unformat features. You'll find similar rescue utilities in PC Tools, and in recent versions of MS-DOS, PC DOS, and Novell DOS. You should have some sort of data-rescue program on hand—and on floppy. (You're likely to need a rescue program precisely when you can't get to it if it's stored only on your hard drive.) But having a rescue utility doesn't absolve you of the three golden rules of computing: back up, back up, and back up. Especially before making any major change in your system, back up. And because backing up large drives to floppy disks is such a time-consuming task, one of the first upgrades you should consider is a tape backup drive.

Although it's nearly impossible to hurt your hardware by using software, there are physical ways in which your computer can be damaged—and one way in which *you* can be damaged. In this section we'll look at those dangers, how to avoid them, and how to recover from them. Through all this, I hope you'll see there's no reason to be afraid of opening up your PC, taking out components and replacing them, or adding new ones. If you take the same reasonable care you would while changing spark plugs, installing a light fixture, or drying the dinner dishes, you're not going to harm your computer.

The following part of the book is devoted to familiarizing you with the main components of your PC—to giving names to all those mysterious chips and circuit boards—and to the simple tools you need to work on your PC. Whenever possible, combine the information you read and see in the illustrations in the book with your own hands-on tour of the insides of your PC. Because of the enormous number of ways in which PCs can be built, the inside of your PC is not going to look exactly like those in these illustrations. The hard drive may be on the opposite side of the case, the memory chips may be hidden beneath the floppy drive, and the speaker may be anywhere. But the illustrations of individual components should be accurate enough for you to identify them in your own system, regardless of location. After you've finished reading the first part of this book, you should know enough about what's inside your PC to perform the upgrades and fixes that I'll cover later on.

I'll also cover the simple precautions you can take to head off damage to your PC. And perhaps most importantly, I'll show you steps that you can take to recover from most PC disasters. The steps are helpful anytime and can save you costly repair bills for simple fixes. But they could prove invaluable when a problem occurs at night, on weekends, or at other times when it isn't practical to call in a repair person. If you skip over any part in this book, don't let it be that one.

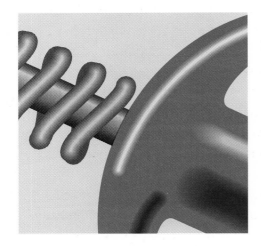

The Tools You Need to Explore Your PC

THE RIGHT TOOLS make any job easier, and when you work with PCs, the tools you need, except for one or two, are not esoteric. If you've done a minimum of household handiwork, you may already have nearly all of the tools you'll need. You can find most of them in any hardware store, but for a few items, you may have to go to a computer retailer or electronics store.

If you can find a collection of computer tools in a neat, zippered case for about $20, buy it. It will contain most of the tools you'll need, and the case is great for keeping all the tools together so that when you need them, you can find them. Don't consider this just a nicety. Later we'll look in greater detail at the need for staying calm in the face of computer disasters. For now, it's enough to say that when something goes wrong with your PC, you don't need the added frustration of not being able to find the one and only tool in the world that will get you out of the bind.

I'm going to discuss some tools here by referring to components and procedures that aren't explained until later in the book. This is a classic chicken-or-the-egg situation, and I've decided to go with the chicken—or is it the egg? Anyway, if you find some terms confusing, please bear with me. It will all be clear soon enough.

Basic Tools

Medium-Sized Flat-Head Screwdriver

Phillips Screwdriver

Torx Screwdriver

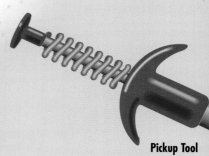

Pickup Tool

Unless your PC is like some that thoughtfully provide knobs you can turn with your fingers to open its case, you'll need at least one of these screwdrivers just to open up your machine. You'll use it to unscrew the sheet-metal screws that hold most PCs together and that secure the expansion cards inside the case.

Most of the screws work with a flat-head screwdriver. Even some Phillips screws can be turned with a flat head if you're desperate. The Torx—or star—screws, best as I can determine, were invented just to make life more difficult and to sell Torx screwdrivers. A Torx screw doesn't hold anything together any more securely that other types of screws, and it's not easier to screw in or unscrew. But all the same you'll find them on some PCs, particularly Compaq-brand units. To match most computer screws, the shaft of flat-head, Phillips, and Torx drivers should measure about ⅜ inch in diameter. A handy variation is a screwdriver with interchangeable heads; you store the heads you're not using in the handle.

Nut Driver

Small Flat-Head Screwdriver

Although having a screwdriver that specifically matches the screws in your PC is a good idea, a hex-nut driver is your best all-around tool for getting into your PC and putting it back together again. A ¼-inch nut driver works with all types of sheetmetal screws—flat-head, Phillips, or Torx—because they all have hexagonal heads. The nut driver is better also because it surrounds the head of the screw, making it less likely that a slip on your part will cause the screw to go flying behind a filing cabinet or that you'll mangle the screwhead with the wrong-size Phillips or flat-head screwdriver. The bolt driver should measure ¼ inch from one side of the hexagon to the opposite side.

This small flat-head screwdriver should measure about ⅛ inch across on its business end. You'll use it primarily to tighten the cables attached to serial, parallel, and other ports. But you'll also find it handy for removing memory chips and setting switches.

Handy Extras

You may not need all of the following, but some of them will come in handy. And when you do need them, the laws of computer repair dictate that it won't be at a time when the hardware stores are open. Look, we're only talking about a few bucks here; get them before you need them.

You can find heavy-duty tweezers at electronic supply stories. I like the cross-lock type pictured here—you squeeze them to release their hold on an object. So, because you don't have to apply pressure, you have greater freedom to manipulate what the tweezers are holding. But the ordinary kind of household tweezers that you use to remove splinters from your finger will do in most situations. Tweezers are helpful if you have to change settings on an expansion board.

Tweezers

Chip Puller

With the predominance of newer memory boards in new PCs, there's less use today for this tool. It was used in the early days of PCs primarily to remove old-fashioned socketed memory chips. (We'll cover this in a later chapter.) Even if you're unlikely to need a chip puller these days, including one in your tool kit will make other computer users think you've been poking around inside PCs for a decade. If you don't have a chip puller, in a pinch you can use the small flat-head screwdriver.

Sooner or later you're going to drop a screw into your PC. It will invariably fall into the tight space between two expansion boards or roll under the motherboard. Unless you turn your PC upside–down and shake it—and you don't really want to do that—you'll need one of these gadgets to retrieve the screw. You use the pickup tool by pushing a knob at one end of a flexible shaft. Four curved claws extend from the other end. You position the claws around whatever you're trying to grab, ease up on the knob, and the claws retract, closing around their victim in the process.

Inspection Mirror

Think of this as a mirror-on-a-stick. It's handy for locating that little screw you dropped. It's also handy for checking the settings on switches that PC makers like to locate in the most inaccessible spot they can find. If your computer is taking a particularly long time on a task, you can also use the mirror to pass the time with personal grooming. [*Continued on the next page.*]

Basic Tools

Handy Extras

These pliers with their long, narrow grippers always come in handy—whether for holding screws until you get them started, removing a floppy disk that's stuck in a drive, or retrieving objects that are too heavy for the pickup tool to handle. In a bind, if you've lost your screwdrivers and nut driver, you can use a needlenose to undo a sheet-metal screw.

Needlenose Pliers

Even if you work on your PC in a clean, well-lighted place, you'll need a penlight to check recessed areas. In particular, it's difficult to see how well expansion boards are seated in their slots because the boards themselves block most work lights. The smaller and lighter a penlight is, the better—you're likely to wind up holding it in your teeth while both your hands are busy. For that same reason, I prefer a plastic case rather than those fashionable high-tech metal penlights. I hate biting down on metal.

Penlight

HOT TIP Magnets are always dangerous to have around floppy disks. If you absentmindedly lay the magnet on a floppy, it will destroy the disk's data. A magnet can also harm hard drives and some motherboard components. Be aware that screwdrivers and pliers are often magnetized. Some are manufactured that way; others just become magnetized by lying next to magnetized tools. Before using a tool on your PC, test it to make sure that it's not magnetized—try to pick up a screw. If it picks up the screw, be sure to store the tool away from floppies.

This comes under a number of brand names, but they're all basically the same—some sort of pressurized gas (not necessarily the same air we breathe) combined with a long plastic nozzle that's handy for getting to inaccessible areas. I find it invaluable not only for cleaning my PC but for giving my desk a quick cleaning to get rid of all those food crumbs. Not all computer supply stores carry canned air. If you have a hard time finding it, check with a photographic supply store. Look for brands that do not use ozone-damaging gases.

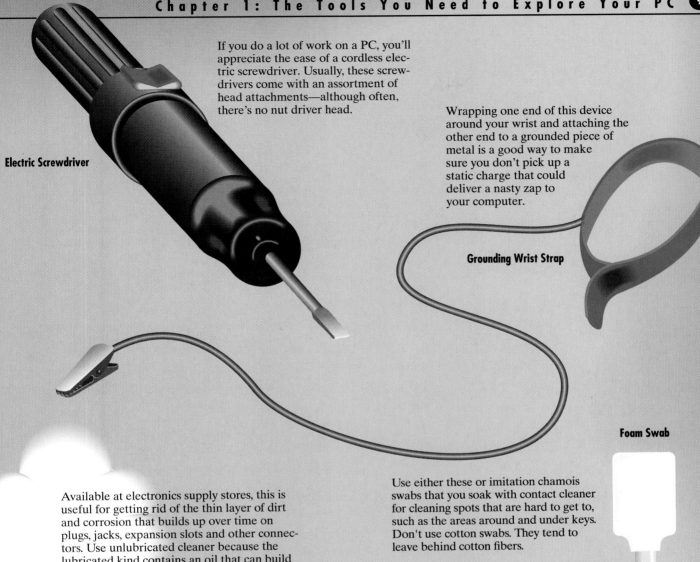

If you do a lot of work on a PC, you'll appreciate the ease of a cordless electric screwdriver. Usually, these screwdrivers come with an assortment of head attachments—although often, there's no nut driver head.

Electric Screwdriver

Wrapping one end of this device around your wrist and attaching the other end to a grounded piece of metal is a good way to make sure you don't pick up a static charge that could deliver a nasty zap to your computer.

Grounding Wrist Strap

Foam Swab

Available at electronics supply stores, this is useful for getting rid of the thin layer of dirt and corrosion that builds up over time on plugs, jacks, expansion slots and other connectors. Use unlubricated cleaner because the lubricated kind contains an oil that can build up and actually attract dirt.

Use either these or imitation chamois swabs that you soak with contact cleaner for cleaning spots that are hard to get to, such as the areas around and under keys. Don't use cotton swabs. They tend to leave behind cotton fibers.

Screen Cleaner

Unlubricated Contact Cleaner

Available in spray cans and presoaked pads, this differs from ordinary window spray because it leaves less film on the screen and it helps prevent the screen building up a static charge, which attracts dust and grime.

SCREEN WIPE

StaticStopper Cleaning Pad

What's Under the Hood?

CRACKING OPEN THE case of your PC to see what's inside can be a great adventure—or a nail-biting torture. The only difference is your attitude. Consider it an adventure, a safe adventure. I'm not going to tell you to do anything that will void your warranty, crash your hard drive, or fry your motherboard—or you.

Personal computers come in two basic styles: desktop and tower. A desktop computer usually rests horizontally on a desk's surface with the monitor on top of it. A tower PC is designed to rest on one of its narrow ends, often under a desk. Its floppy and CD drives are positioned so that their disk openings are horizontal, as on a desktop computer.

For our illustrations, in most instances, we'll be showing a desktop PC. There is no functional difference between the two types, but you can usually add more expansion cards and drives to a tower PC. If your PC is a tower system, all the illustrations and instructions in the following chapters still apply. You may simply have to perform a little mental gymnastics at times to imagine an illustration turned on its side.

There is no reason, by the way, that you can't turn a desktop unit on its side and put it on the floor. At one time, some argued that hard drives were designed to be mounted horizontally, and turning a desktop PC on its side could lead to a hard drive failure. But I've never heard of this happening, and I've used several desktop PCs standing on end with no problems. If you do this, you should make sure that the PC is not likely to fall over. One way to ensure stability is to use a brace specially designed to provide a bigger footprint for a desktop PC placed on its side, as shown here.

A big chunk of your PC's insides is devoted to the *power supply*, which acts as a mediator between the electricity coming out of the wall socket and the components that consume that electricity. The *motherboard* is the large printed-circuit board, usually green, that stretches across the base of the computer. (In a tower PC, the motherboard is, of course, mounted vertically.) The motherboard contains most of the chips that do the basic computing and the chips that make up the *random access memory*, or RAM, which is where programs are loaded when they're being used. The programs also use RAM as a temporary scratch pad for the data they're working with. Plugged into special connectors on the motherboard are several *expansion cards* that perform specialized jobs, such as controlling the monitor display or disk drives. On some PCs, the functions performed by expansion cards are built directly into the motherboard, which means that you may not find in your PC all the expansion cards illustrated on this brief tour.

Cracking the Case

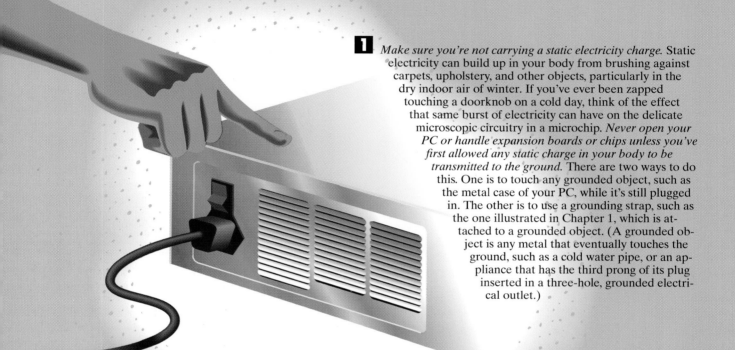

1 *Make sure you're not carrying a static electricity charge.* Static electricity can build up in your body from brushing against carpets, upholstery, and other objects, particularly in the dry indoor air of winter. If you've ever been zapped touching a doorknob on a cold day, think of the effect that same burst of electricity can have on the delicate microscopic circuitry in a microchip. *Never open your PC or handle expansion boards or chips unless you've first allowed any static charge in your body to be transmitted to the ground.* There are two ways to do this. One is to touch any grounded object, such as the metal case of your PC, while it's still plugged in. The other is to use a grounding strap, such as the one illustrated in Chapter 1, which is attached to a grounded object. (A grounded object is any metal that eventually touches the ground, such as a cold water pipe, or an appliance that has the third prong of its plug inserted in a three-hole, grounded electrical outlet.)

2 Turn off your PC and unplug the power cord from the back of the PC. Make a habit of unplugging it there rather than at the wall—for two reasons: The plug is often easier to reach at the back of the PC than at the wall, and the number of PC components that are likely to proliferate around your system makes it likely that you could unplug something else by mistake. *After you're grounded, make this the first step you perform whenever you start to repair your PC, add a component, or just examine the inside. You risk danger to yourself and your system if you open your PC while it's still plugged in.*

3 Locate the screws that secure the cover of your PC's case. On a desktop model, there are usually three to five screws located along the perimeter of the case. On a tower model, there may be as many as eight or ten. Use a screwdriver or hexnut driver to undo the machine screws.

4 Remove the case. For many PCs, both desktop and tower, this involves sliding the cover toward the rear of the computer before you can lift it away.

HOT TIP Those little screws that hold onto the case and hold in expansion cards have a life of their own and will scamper away to get lost as soon as you turn your back. When you remove the screws, tape them to the case for safekeeping.

Hiker's Guide to the Inside of the PC

Expansion slots are used to hold expansion cards, or adapters, which expand the capabilities of your PC. Typical expansion cards include the video adapter and the disk controller, athough the function of these cards is built into the motherboard on some PCs. If your expansion slots don't look exactly like the ones here, that's because there are currently six different types of slots (covered in detail in a later chapter).

ROM BIOS chips, when the computer is turned on, hold the basic code to start operations until an operating system can be loaded from a disk. ROM, or *read-only memory*, means the code in the BIOS chips can be read by the PC, but it cannot be changed. BIOS stands for *basic input/output system*. The BIOS is used by the operating system to input (receive) and output (send) data from and to hardware devices such as disk drives and the keyboard. Some hardware devices, for example, video cards, may have their own BIOS chips that let the operating system communicate with them.

The internal speaker is adequate only for beeps. It's not the speaker a multimedia PC uses.

RAM (random access memory) is where programs are loaded and where data is held while the processor is manipulating it. When you turn off your PC or reboot it, anything that is stored in RAM is lost.

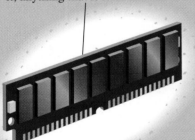

The clock chip regulates the speed, expressed in megahertz (MHz), at which your PC processes data. You can determine the speed of your PC from a number printed on the chip. If the number you find doesn't match the standard speeds—16MHz, 25 MHz, 33MHz, 50MHz, 66MHz—try dividing by 2.

The CMOS battery provides enough of a small electrical charge to let the CMOS chip retain its memory when the PC is turned off. It must be replaced every few years.

The CMOS chip retains a record of the hardware installed in your PC—for example, the number and type of hard drives and the amount of memory. The information is kept alive by a small battery while the PC is turned off.

The hard drive is the primary storage device. Data and programs saved to the hard drive are retained when the PC is turned off.

The floppy drive, in function, is similar to a hard drive. Floppy disks inserted into the drive can store programs and data permanently. But a floppy drive cannot store as much data as a hard drive can, and it is slower when it comes to storing or retrieving data.

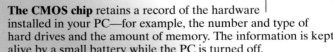

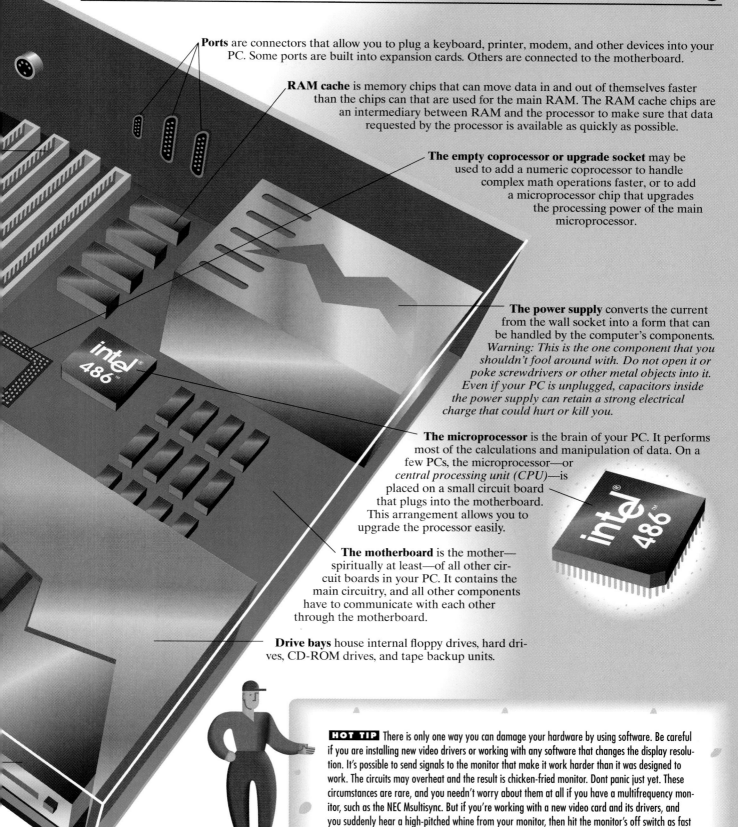

Ports are connectors that allow you to plug a keyboard, printer, modem, and other devices into your PC. Some ports are built into expansion cards. Others are connected to the motherboard.

RAM cache is memory chips that can move data in and out of themselves faster than the chips can that are used for the main RAM. The RAM cache chips are an intermediary between RAM and the processor to make sure that data requested by the processor is available as quickly as possible.

The empty coprocessor or upgrade socket may be used to add a numeric coprocessor to handle complex math operations faster, or to add a microprocessor chip that upgrades the processing power of the main microprocessor.

The power supply converts the current from the wall socket into a form that can be handled by the computer's components. *Warning: This is the one component that you shouldn't fool around with. Do not open it or poke screwdrivers or other metal objects into it. Even if your PC is unplugged, capacitors inside the power supply can retain a strong electrical charge that could hurt or kill you.*

The microprocessor is the brain of your PC. It performs most of the calculations and manipulation of data. On a few PCs, the microprocessor—or *central processing unit (CPU)*—is placed on a small circuit board that plugs into the motherboard. This arrangement allows you to upgrade the processor easily.

The motherboard is the mother— spiritually at least—of all other circuit boards in your PC. It contains the main circuitry, and all other components have to communicate with each other through the motherboard.

Drive bays house internal floppy drives, hard drives, CD-ROM drives, and tape backup units.

HOT TIP There is only one way you can damage your hardware by using software. Be careful if you are installing new video drivers or working with any software that changes the display resolution. It's possible to send signals to the monitor that make it work harder than it was designed to work. The circuits may overheat and the result is chicken-fried monitor. Dont panic just yet. These circumstances are rare, and you needn't worry about them at all if you have a multifrequency monitor, such as the NEC Msultisync. But if you're working with a new video card and its drivers, and you suddenly hear a high-pitched whine from your monitor, then hit the monitor's off switch as fast as you can.

CHAPTER 3

You and Your New PC

HERE'S THE GOOD news: That new personal computer you just bought—or you're thinking of buying—is a hardy, resilient piece of machinery. You almost have to go out of your way to break it.

Here's the bad news: When trouble does happen, it invariably comes at the least convenient time. The last chapter of this book, "The Midnight Drill," focuses on the steps you can take to recover from a hardware disaster when the normal sources of rescue—service technicians, the store that sold you the PC, and friendly computer gurus—aren't available. It's the last chapter because a lot of it will only make sense if you've already explored your PC through some of the earlier chapters. But if you're in trouble now, don't stand on formalities. Skip straight to the last chapter and fill in gaps in the information with selected reading of the chapters between here and there.

But if you have a new PC, you can do a lot to prevent ever having to read that last chapter by how you set up your PC from the very start. Sure, you're anxious to begin using it, and it is under warranty and all, but here's a tip: You don't want to use that warranty. Warranty repairs take a long time. You may have to ship your PC to another city. Even if the service is done locally, you're going to be without a PC for at least a couple of days. Plus, some of the advice you follow now will help you to avoid repairs later when the warranty has expired. Wait until after the warranty period to follow this advice, and you may have waited too long.

Most computer malfunctions are caused by heat and bad connections. In this chapter, starting from the time you take your PC out of the box, we'll look at some of the steps you should take to avoid overheating and other forms of trouble down the line.

The first step is to *burn in* your PC. Burning in a computer is based on the idea that nearly all defective components will reveal their flaws in the first several hours of use. That's because almost all flaws are caused by heat. Some minuscule defect in the materials used to create microchips and circuit boards causes a breakdown after the PC has run for several hours, during which all the components heat up. If the components survive the first 72 hours of use, then they're likely to last indefinitely.

A reputable manufacturer burns in its PCs for at least 72 hours. Some even put circuit boards into a giant oven, where they're cooked for hours at temperatures higher than they'll ever encounter in real-world use. But even if you have explicit trust in the company that built your PC, conduct your own 72-hour burn in. And add one element that most other burn ins neglect. Every couple of hours or so, turn off your PC and let it cool off completely—about a half hour should do it. Then turn it back on for a few more hours. The heating and cooling cause components to expand and contract. In some rare instances, this can make chips work loose in their sockets. (I once owned a computer that made a career of this defect. About once a month, I had to open the case and push several of the chips back into their sockets. With some of the chips, I could hear audible *pops* as they reseated.)

Obviously, you want any defect to show up while your PC is still under warranty. But ideally, you want a defect to show up within a few days. That makes it easier to demand that the seller completely replace the system with a new one rather than go the more arduous route of warranty repair.

Try to calm your baser instincts to jump right into computing. The time you spend setting up your PC now can save you a lot of grief later when you need to make repairs or upgrade the system. Some of the advice in this chapter can even prevent the need for some repairs to your system later.

The following illustration shows you safer procedures for setting up a computer for the first time.

Setup Do's and Don'ts

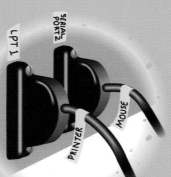

**DON'T just plug in
your cables.**

DO identify cables.
When you have half a dozen
or more cables, all looking
pretty much the same, it's difficult to trace a cable from a
port on your PC to the printer,
modem, or other peripheral to
which it's connected. Label your cables
at both ends; some tape and an indelible
marker will do the job and save you time and work
later when you're trouble-shooting a cabling problem.

**DON'T leave your
modem unprotected.**
**DO use a modem
surge protector.**
One computer component that too often
gets overlooked when it comes to surge
protection is the modem. Even if an external modem is plugged into a surge protector, lightning that strikes a phone line can
enter the modem that way and destroy it.
(Believe me—this happens. I had two
modems zapped during thunderstorms.)
Look for a surge protector that, in addition
to power cord connectors, includes phone
line connections. They're hard to find; or
you could go with a small, dedicated phone
line surge protector sold by Radio Shack
(catalog number, 43–102A).

DON'T leave connectors loose.
DO tighten screws on connectors.
Cords invariable get moved when you attach new cords,
shift your monitor around, move your keyboard or stretch
your legs under your desk. If the connections aren't screwed
down tight, you'll suddenly find you can't print or that your
PC is complaining that it can't detect your modem. If you
have a choice in buying cables, get the kind that have screw-
down connectors that you can turn with your fingers, instead
of using a screwdriver.

DON'T create cable clutter.
DO use cable ties.
The cables that connect your PC with its modem, printer,
electrical outlet, mouse, and all the other peripherals you're
likely to add have a mysterious ability to become entangled
no matter how you try to avoid it. Use cable ties to bundle
several of the cables together and to hold excess cable from
a single connector in a loop. I like the reusable cable ties
sold by Radio Shack (catalog number 278–1622) because
they can be undone without having to cut the ties. You'll be
thankful for the organization later when you're in the
middle of a frustrating job of trying to track down a bad
connection or if you must disconnect all your cables to
move your PC.

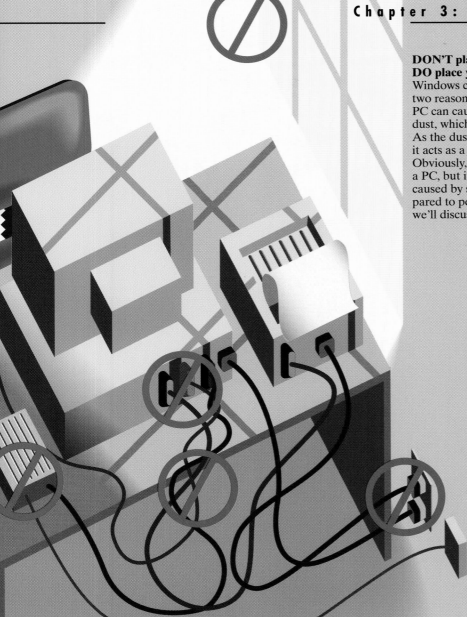

DON'T place your PC in a sunny spot or dusty area.
DO place your PC in a cool location.
Windows can be hazardous to the health of your PC for
two reasons: Sunlight shining through a window on your
PC can cause it to overheat, and an open window invites
dust, which can be sucked into your PC by its cooling fan.
As the dust accumulates on chips and over components,
it acts as a blanket and may cause them to overheat.
Obviously, a climate-controlled room is the best place for
a PC, but if you don't have that, avoid obvious hot spots
caused by sunlight. And if you're a fresh air fan, be prepared to perform more often the maintenance procedures
we'll discuss later in the book.

DON'T use ungrounded outlets.
DO make sure your PC is grounded.
This grounded electrical outlet has
two narrow vertical slots, plus a half-
rounded third slot for the ground
prong on the PC power cord. If your
office or home doesn't have grounded
outlets, have one installed by a li-
censed electrician. Don't use an
adapter that allows three-prong plugs
to plug into a two-prong outlet. These
adapters are supposed to add grounding, but whether they actually do depends on how the original outlet was
installed. Don't take a chance.

DON'T plug directly into the wall outlet.
DO use a Surge Protector.
Before you ever turn on your PC for the first time, you should first plug it into a *spike*
or *surge protector*. This is a device that protects your PC from an excessive dose of
electricity that can travel from your electrical outlet into your PC and fry its components. The surge can come from a bolt of lightning or simply from fluctuations in
your neighborhood's power grid. The most common form of surge protector is a
combination extension cord and multiple outlets. But not everything that looks like
this is a surge protector; some units are just expensive extension cords with no protection. A good surge protector will cost between $20 and $30 and have a light that
indicates that the surge protector is functioning. The light is important. If the surge
protector takes several even minor hits, its components that protect your PC can
become worn out themselves. They literally sacrifice their own lives to save your PC.
If your surge protector does not have a pilot light, it should be replaced every six
months to a year in case it has taken fatal hits you don't know about.

CHAPTER 4

Preparing for an Emergency

SOMEDAY, SOMETHING WILL go wrong with your PC. The hard drive may take a nose dive. A message may appear saying something mysterious about your PC's memory and a parity error. Your PC may simply refuse to come to life. Whatever happens, you're better off if you've prepared by keeping a record of what is installed in your PC. Fixing your computer may depend on knowing the exact technical description of your hard drive or how much memory you have.

Even if a disaster doesn't strike your PC—yeah, sure—there are two other times when you want to know exactly what type of hardware you have and how it's set up. One is when you experience what seems to be a software problem. Among the first questions someone on a technical support phone line is going to ask is how much memory you have, what type of processor, and what other hardware you have that could affect how the software works. The other time you'll want to know what you've got is when you start to install a new component—an expansion card, a new drive, or more memory. Hardly anything in your PC works in a vacuum. Each of its components depends on a harmonious relationship with all the other components. If, for example, two expansion cards both try to use the same chunk of memory at the same time, neither of them will work right.

It's not a good time to figure out the contents of your system when your PC has crashed, or when you've got tech support on the other end of a long-distance phone call, or when you're anxious to play with that new sound card. But now is a good time—when you're calm, when nothing's wrong, when you're got plenty of time.

Now is also the time to make an emergency boot disk. One of the Catch 22s of computing is that when something goes wrong so that you can't get to files on your hard drive, some of the software that might let you fix the problem is—guess where—on the hard drive. Sometimes you don't even care if you can fix the hard drive immediately. You'd be happy if you could move one file—just one file—from the hard drive to a floppy so that you could continue working with it on another PC.

When you boot, or turn on, your PC, it can't do anything else until it's copied several files from the hard drive to memory. These are the system files that make up the operating system. The operating system is, in turn, what lets you run software applications, such as word processors or databases. Occasionally, something may happen to only the hard drive's system files. Through pure chance, the part of the hard drive that contains the system files may develop a physical defect, or some unruly software may change the system files. Or through sheer malice, a software virus could mangle the system files. In any of these situations, you might be able to use your applications or at least transfer the files you need to a floppy if you could only boot your computer.

An emergency boot disk is a floppy for your A drive; it contains all the files you need to get your PC working when you can't boot from the hard drive. It's a simple enough precaution, but it's one you have to do now. If you wait until you need it, you're too late.

The rest of this chapter will show you how to find out what's in your PC and how to create a floppy boot disk. When you finish the chapter, you can consider yourself fully armed with tools, information, and an emergency kit, and prepared to tackle the tasks of fixing or upgrading your PC.

CMOS Setup Screens

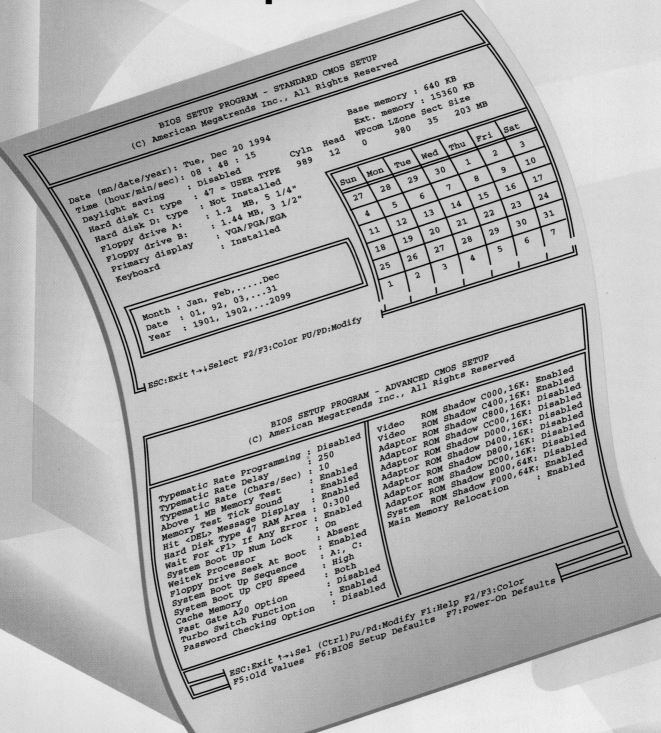

```
            BIOS SETUP PROGRAM - STANDARD CMOS SETUP          Base memory : 640 KB
              (C) American Megatrends Inc., All Rights Reserved    Ext. memory : 15360 KB
                                                          WPcom LZone Sect Size
                                          Cyln  Head     0    980    35    203 MB
  Date (mn/date/year): Tue, Dec 20 1994    989   12
  Time (hour/min/sec): 08 : 48 : 15
  Daylight saving        : Disabled               Sun  Mon  Tue  Wed  Thu  Fri  Sat
  Hard disk C: type      : 47 = USER TYPE                          30    1    2    3
  Hard disk D: type      : Not Installed          27   28   29          8    9   10
  Floppy drive A:        : 1.2  MB, 5 1/4"                          7
  Floppy drive B:        : 1.44 MB, 3 1/2"         4    5    6         15   16   17
  Primary display        : VGA/PGA/EGA                             14
  Keyboard               : Installed              11   12   13         22   23   24
                                                                  21
                                                 18   19   20         29   30   31
                                                                  28
                                                 25   26   27          5    6    7
  Month : Jan, Feb,.....Dec                                        4
  Date  : 01, 92, 03,...31                         1    2    3               6    7
  Year  : 1901, 1902,...2099                                        5

  ESC:Exit ↑→↓Select F2/F3:Color PU/PD:Modify
```

```
            BIOS SETUP PROGRAM - ADVANCED CMOS SETUP
              (C) American Megatrends Inc., All Rights Reserved
                                                        Video    ROM Shadow C000,16K: Enabled
                                                        Video    ROM Shadow C400,16K: Enabled
  Typematic Rate Programming : Disabled              Adaptor ROM Shadow C800,16K: Disabled
  Typematic Rate Delay         : 250                 Adaptor ROM Shadow CC00,16K: Disabled
  Typematic Rate (Chars/Sec)   : 10                  Adaptor ROM Shadow D000,16K: Disabled
  Above 1 MB Memory Test       : Enabled             Adaptor ROM Shadow D400,16K: Disabled
  Memory Test Tick Sound       : Enabled             Adaptor ROM Shadow D800,16K: Disabled
  Hit <DEL> Message Display    : Enabled             Adaptor ROM Shadow DC00,16K: Disabled
  Hard Disk Type 47 RAM Area   : 0:300               Adaptor ROM Shadow E000,64K: Enabled
  Wait For <F1> If Any Error   : Enabled             System  ROM Shadow F000,64K: Enabled
  System Boot Up Num Lock      : On                  Main Memory Relocation      : Enabled
  Weitek Processor             : Absent
  Floppy Drive Seek At Boot    : Enabled
  System Boot Up Sequence      : A:, C:
  System Boot Up CPU Speed     : High
  Cache Memory                 : Both
  Fast Gate A20 Option         : Disabled
  Turbo Switch Function        : Enabled
  Password Checking Option     : Disabled

  ESC:Exit ↑→↓Sel (Ctrl)Pu/Pd:Modify F1:Help F2/F3:Color
  F5:Old Values  F6:BIOS Setup Defaults  F7:Power-On Defaults
```

Your PC and MS–DOS, the operating system that is mostly likely the one that your PC uses, provides the two tools that supply most of the information you need to create a record of the inside of your PC. With these tools—the CMOS setup program built into your computer and Microsoft Diagnostics, or MSD.EXE—you can create a printed record of almost everything that's in your PC and how it's all configured.

This printout on the facing page shows the CMOS configuration for my PC. It contains a lot of information that's not very interesting, such as the system date and time. And it contains a lot of information that you're better off never getting near, such as settings for a crucial part of your system called a RAM cache. But the most crucial piece of information is the type of hard drive. Each hard drive has a different number of cylinders, heads, tracks, and sectors per track. If the information in your CMOS doesn't match the physical characteristics of your hard drive, your PC may refuse to write or read files to the disk or it may write files improperly, leading to big problems later.

Even if you don't change any of the components in your PC, if you keep your personal computer long enough, you'll encounter one situation in which you'll need a record of your CMOS setup. That's when you have to change the battery for the CMOS chip. The chip retains the data recorded on it as long as it receives a small trickle of electricity from a battery. It preserves crucial information about your PC while it's turned off. After a couple of years or so, you'll have to replace this battery. (One of the first signs that your battery is failing is when the system's time and date start to change on their own.) Replacing the battery means that you'll have to disconnect power to the CMOS chip, however fleetingly, and during this time, the information stored in the CMOS will be lost.

The CMOS screen is activated differently on different PCs, but they have one characteristic in common: The screens usually can be activated in the time between when you flip the power switch on and when the operating system is loaded. During that time, you can usually press some combination of keys, such as Del, F1, or Ctrl-Alt-S, to bring up the CMOS screen. Sometimes your computer screen tells you which keys to press; otherwise you'll have to check the manual that came with your PC. That is the way that you access the CMOS screen with most PCs. But if you have a PC with an EISA, MCA, or Plug-and-Play bus, then you may have to run a utility program supplied with your computer to access the CMOS screen.

After you activate the CMOS setup, the simplest way to make a record of it is to use the PrintScreen key (labelled PrtScrn on some keyboards). Make sure your printer is turned on and press Shift-PrintScreen or Alt-Shift-PrintScreen. You'll see the printer's form-feed light come on, indicating that the printer has received the screen's text and is waiting for you to press the form-feed button to eject the page. But don't press the button just yet. You can fit two screen dumps on a single page. So if your CMOS setup has more than one screen, press PageDown or whatever key takes you to the next screen, and use the PrintScreen key again. Now press the form-feed button. If you have still more screens in your CMOS setup, repeat the process until you have a printed record of everything in your CMOS. This does not work with a PostScript printer.

MSD.EXE includes much of the same information you'll find in the CMOS setup screens. To see what MSD has to say about your system, let's try the utility right now. If you're running Windows, you must first exit Windows and get back to the DOS prompt (C:>). If MSD is run under Windows, it can only report what information Windows provides it, and Windows plays tricks with your system's memory. At the DOS prompt, type **MSD** and press the Enter key. If you get a "bad command or file name" message, change to the directory in which you have all your DOS files and try again.

Snooping with MSD.EXE

The Opening Screen of MSD (Microsoft Diagnostics)

The screen to the left lets you select among several components to find out how they're configured. After spending a few seconds investigating your system, MSD will display the opening screen shown. Explore the information MSD can provide by selecting some of the menu items. Those that will be most useful later as you install new hardware or troubleshoot problems will be Memory, IRQ Status, TSR Programs, and Device Drivers.

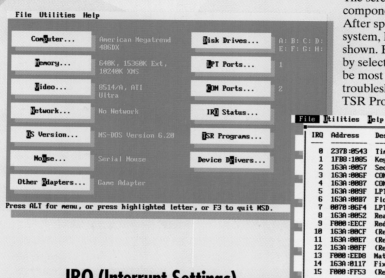

IRQ (Interrupt Settings) Displayed on a MSD Screen

The screen to the right shows IRQ settings. It's important to have the information provided by both your CMOS setup and MSD. The IRQ status, TSR programs, and device drivers are details of your system that are not included in the CMOS screens because they don't take effect until the operating system is loaded, which is not possible before displaying a CMOS screen.

MSD's Report on the Hard Drive

This report may give apparently conflicting figures. Believe the hard drive information you get from the CMOS screen. On the other hand, MSD may report information that is incorrect or confusing. For example, the MSD examination on drives for my system shown below reports two different cylinder, head, and sector/track settings for each of my drives. The reason for the apparent discrepancy is that I've divided my physical drives into smaller logical drives. (A *physical drive* is just that, the hunk of hardware in your machine. A *logical drive* is what your operating system thinks is out there. You can take one physical drive—for example, drive C—and by using a utility supplied with DOS, make your system treat only half of the space on the drive as if it were drive C and the rest of the space as if it were a separate D drive. These fictitious drives are called *logical drives*.) In my case, the problem is complicated further by the fact that I have used a program called Stacker to increase the amount of data I can save on my drives.

In addition, the CMOS contains information on some very fundamental operations involving memory. These are settings that MSD knows nothing about. In most instances, you shouldn't change these advanced CMOS factory settings. But you should have a printed record of them.

You should print the information provided by MSD. It has a built-in printing option you can access by pressing **Alt, File, Print**. You'll be presented with the screen you see to the right. You should print all the options it presents at least once. If you have WIN.INI and SYSTEM.INI, make sure your printer's well stocked with paper. My complete printout runs 47 pages. If you eliminate all the files in the last column from AUTOEXEC.BAT down, you'll have a more manageable nine pages of core information about your system.

It's not enough to have records of your system setup and your AUTOEXEC.BAT and CONFIG.SYS files on paper. You need to have some files and information on a floppy disk. There may come a day when you turn on your PC and encounter a message saying that the C drive is not valid or not a system disk. Through accident or mischief, something has happened to the CMOS settings or to the system files that load the operating system. And without the CMOS setup and operating system, your PC is a big, rather unattractive paperweight.

You should always keep a floppy disk for your A drive that contains the system files plus any device driver files needed for various hardware components to work and some tools that you hope will let you fix the problem. Here are the steps to create a boot disk.

1. Insert a new, blank floppy disk in your A drive, and from the C:> prompt, type the command **FORMAT A: /S** and press the Enter key. Your PC will take a minute or so while it formats the disk and transfers the system files to it. If you examine the floppy after it's formatted, you'll see only one file, COMMAND.COM, but there are two other files that are saved with a hidden attribute so that they don't crop up on directory lists. All together the three files make up the core of the DOS operating system.

2. Now use the COPY command to copy AUTOEXEC.BAT and CONFIG.SYS from drive C to the floppy in drive A. Then use the DOS text editor to open the copy of CONFIG.SYS on drive A (EDIT A:\CONFIG.SYS). Look for lines that load device drivers or other programs, basically anything with an equals sign and a file name, such as:

```
DEVICE= C:\DOS\HIMEM.SYS
SHELL=C:\DOS\COMMAND.COM C:\DOS\ /P
DEVICE=C:\STACKER\STACKER.COM C:\STACVOL.DSK
DEVICE=C:\SMARTDRV.EXE /DOUBLE_BUFFER
```

3. Make a notation of the files and their directories and then use EDIT's Search/Change feature to change every instance of C: that follows an equals sign to A:. (You don't want to change, for example, the second C: in the line above that includes the STACKER command.) Save the file. Now using your notes about the files in the CONFIG.SYS lines, use the XCOPY command with an /S switch to copy each of the files to the A drive. XCOPY used with the /S switch at the end of the command line copies not only the file, but the directory structure that contains the file. For example:

```
XCOPY C:\DOS\HIMEM.SYS A: /S
XCOPY C:\DOS\COMMAND.COM A: /S
XCOPY C:\STACKER\STACKER.COM A: /S
XCOPY C:\SMARTDRV.EXE A: /S
```

4. Follow the same steps with your AUTOEXEC.BAT file. Depending on what trouble has forced you to resort to using a boot floppy, some of the commands, such as STACKER, which compresses files to get more of them on a disk, may not do you any good. But if, for example, you're the victim of a computer virus that has attacked only the C drive's boot files, then a boot floppy will let you copy the data files—documents and spreadsheets—to another floppy and use a different PC to get vital work done.

5. Include on your boot floppy some utility programs that can help correct disk troubles. The utilities CHKDSK.EXE, SCANDISK.EXE, SYS.COM, FORMAT.EXE, FDISK.EXE, UNFORMAT.COM, and UNDELETE.EXE all provided with MS-DOS, should be on the floppy. But as helpful as those programs are, you need some higher-caliber ammunition, such as Norton Disk Doctor from the Norton Utilities and a good virus eradication program. (I prefer Dr. Solomon's Anti-Virus.)

Emergency boot disk

File Utilities Help

```
Report Information
[ ] Report All          [X] Mouse           [X] Memory Browser
[X] Customer Information [X] Other Adapters  [X] CONFIG.SYS
[X] System Summary      [X] Disk Drives     [X] AUTOEXEC.BAT
[X] Computer            [X] LPT Ports       [X] WIN.INI
[X] Memory              [X] COM Ports       [X] SYSTEM.INI
[X] Video               [X] IRQ Status
[X] Network             [X] TSR Programs
[X] DOS Version         [X] Device Drivers

Print to:
(•) LPT1  ( ) COM1      ( ) COM4
( ) LPT2  ( ) COM2      ( ) File: [REPORT.MSD....................]
( ) LPT3  ( ) COM3

              OK      Cancel
```

Other Adapters...

Prints a report to a printer or a file.

THANKS FOR THE MEMORY

CONTENTS

AT THE CORE OF all computers—from the little idiot savant computers in your watch and microwave oven to the giant computers that predict the paths of space-craft—there is memory. It's not inaccurate to think of a computer as nothing but memory. Those parts that aren't memory themselves exist to aid memory—to help memory get it-self organized, to change what's in memory, to get new information into memory, and to display what's already in memory. The microprocessor that's at the heart of a PC is de-voted to juggling the data contained in several tiny pieces of memory called *registers.* As the name of a once-popular brand of floppy disks—Elephant—emphasized, hard and floppy disks are simply a more permanent form of memory, one that, when you turn off the power, doesn't forget everything as does the more fragile memory called *RAM,* or random access memory.

RAM is usually what we mean when we talk about a computer's memory. RAM consists of a handful of microchips that contain thousands or millions of microscopic switches. Whether a switch is turned off or on determines if it represents a 0 or a 1. Those 0s and 1s, in turn, function as binary numbers and represent all data, from words to pho-tographs to the decimal numbers that we're more familiar with. In the binary system, 1 represents 1, but decimal 2 is 10, 3 is 11, 4 is 100, 5 is 101, and so on.

There are other forms of memory chips. The *basic input/output system,* or BIOS—a chunk of code that defines how your software interacts with your hardware and lets your PC boot in the first place—is stored in one or two chips called ROM, read-only memory. ROM doesn't lose its contents when the computer is turned off, but neither can the con-tents be changed. Another type of memory chip, CMOS memory, can be written to and when your PC is turned off, a small battery prevents the CMOS chip from losing its contents—a detailed description of the hardware in your system.

Various expansion cards contain their own memory chips. The video card has mem-ory chips that contain a record of what is to be displayed on screen. When your software changes the display, it actually does that by changing the contents of the video memory. Memory chips may be on the expansion card that controls your drives; there they help move data faster from your drive to RAM. And most newer PCs have a *RAM cache,* which is a collection of very fast, expensive memory chips that help move data faster from ordinary RAM to the processor.

Generally it's RAM—plain, ordinary RAM—that most concerns us and that we can do something to improve. You can replace the RAM chips you have with faster or more capacious RAM, or simply add similar chips to the ones you already have. And you prob-ably should because, of all the parts of your PC, RAM is the one that can most affect the overall performance and ease of use of your PC.

It wasn't always that way. The assumption of software programmers in the ancient days of the PC (circa 1981) was that any computer running their programs wasn't going to have much memory. Programmers then prided themselves on writing compact programs that could fit on one floppy disk and run in 64K of RAM.

At the time, the memory used for programs in a PC running Microsoft DOS could, in theory, be raised to as much as 640K, but computer experts of the day stated flatly that no one would ever need that much memory. And that's why the limitation exists. It was easier to create an operating system with a relatively simple method of handling memory if all it had to deal with was 640K for programs, plus several hundred more kilobytes reserved for the used of video cards, disk controllers, and other hardware. The experts and the programmers were, of course, as wrong as they could be about how generous 640K was. Soon 640K became, not some elusive, theoretical limitation, but a brick wall that brought development of more powerful software to a squealing halt.

Today, the 640K barrier is crumbling. New operating environments, such as Windows and OS/2, can handle memory several dozen times larger than 640K. In fact, they demand more memory for optimum performance. A minimum of 2 megabytes (MB) is required just to run these modern operating environments, but the performance is utterly unsatisfactory. Some Windows applications require a minimum of 4MB of memory, but even with that much RAM, more complex software applications run so slow as to drive you to distraction. My own recommendation is that you don't try to run Windows with less than 6MB of RAM; 8MB is even better.

Here's why memory makes so much difference in Windows performance. One of the advantages of Windows is that you can run more than one program at a time. With a click of the mouse or a couple keystrokes, you can switch to any of them instantly—instantly, that is, if you have enough memory. If you don't have enough real memory, then Windows makes use of something called virtual memory. Under the virtual-memory scheme, Windows treats a portion of your hard disk as if it were RAM. When Windows runs out of real RAM in which to run a program, it copies some other program in RAM to virtual memory on the hard drive. If you later need to use the program that's in virtual memory, Windows copies some other program to another part of virtual memory and copies the program you want from the disk back into active RAM. Because drives are the slowest part of any PC, all this swapping to and from the hard drive stalls your PC and your work. The more real RAM you have, the less Windows is dependent on virtual RAM and the faster your programs run.

CHAPTER 5

Identifying Your Memory Chips

ADDING MEMORY to your PC is one of the most satisfying and dramatic improvements you can make. But there's a catch. You can't use just any memory chip to increase the amount of your RAM. The memory chips you add must match the capacity of the memory chips you already have and be at least as fast. You can't simply insert only one chip; instead, you may have to insert a certain number of chips—two or eight or nine—at the same time. But all this is not difficult once you learn how to interpret the numbers stamped on memory chips.

The memory that makes up RAM is *DRAM*, or *dynamic random access memory*. It's a relatively inexpensive and not particularly fast type of RAM chip. In PCs built before 1989, the main memory consists of chips called *dual in-line packages*, or *DIP*s. These small, rectangular black chips, with rows of metal legs down each long side, plug into special sockets on the motherboard. Some expansion cards, such as video adapters, also have a fast variety of DIP chips, called VRAM. If you have some empty sockets on your video card, you may be able to improve its performance by adding more memory chips.

More recent personal computers have adopted a new kind of memory, the *single in-line memory module* or *SIMM*. A SIMM is not a chip but is actually a tiny circuit board on which are soldered three to eighteen smaller DIP chips. The little circuit board has metal connectors along one edge that fit into a slot similar to, but smaller than, an expansion slot. A SIMM variation that is found occasionally is called a *SIP*, for *single in-line package*. SIPs are different from SIMMs: Instead of having metal connectors that wrap around the edges of their circuit boards, SIPs have rows of pins that are inserted into sockets. Both SIMMs and SIPs are easier to install than DIPs are because, instead of installing up to nine DIPs, you can install one circuit board containing those nine DIPs and get the same results.

No matter what kind of RAM populates your computer, it has no secrets from you if you know how to read the numbers stamped on the chips. This chapter will show you how to learn enough about the memory chips that you already have so that you can buy chips that are compatible with them in capacity and speed.

Identifying Memory Chips

Finding Your RAM Chips

On older PCs that have DIP chips, the RAM chips are usually located in sockets on the motherboard, laid out in several rows called *banks*. Each bank usually contains eight or nine chips. If there are nine chips, eight of them are used for storing data, and the ninth is what's called a *parity chip*, used to check the other eight chips to make sure they're working right.

DIP chips are small, rectangular chips that have eight metal pins along each side. The pins plug into sockets that are permanently soldered to the motherboard.

SIMMs and SIPs, located on the motherboard, are plugged into rows of small plastic sockets.

SIMMs and SIPs usually have two to nine DIP chips permanently soldered to a small strip of circuit board. (Three, eight, and nine are the most common combinations; the more chips, the more expensive the SIMM/SIP.) At the bottom of the circuit strip are 30 or 72 connectors, or pins, that plug into the plastic sockets.

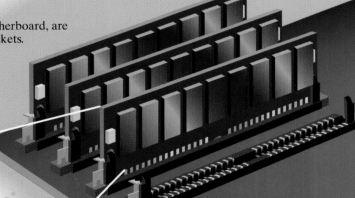

Reading DIP, SIMM, and SIP Chips

The key to determining the capacity and speed of your memory chips is reading the part number information printed on each of the chips. If you're looking at a single DIP chip, the information is on the face of the chip. If you're looking at a SIMM or SIP, the information is on each of the DIP chips attached to the strip of circuit board.

Brand doesn't matter. You can mix and match different brands of chips.

Capacity can be determined by the part number; disregard any letters. Look for exponential values of 2—64, 128, 256—and the numbers 1, 10, 100, and 1000. The exponential values of 2 translate directly to the total capacity of the chips—64K, 128K, 256K. The 10 multiples stand for 1MB. But the capacity does not refer to a single chip; it indicates the amount of memory contained in one bank of DIP chips or an entire SIMM or SIP.

To determine how many chips you need to install at one time, you can sometimes check the number preceding the capacity number you've found. A *1* in front of the capacity number often means that it takes 9 of the chips to add up to the total capacity. But some of these schemes defy logic. A simpler way to figure out how many chips of a certain type you need is to count the number of sockets in one bank of RAM. You will always need to add DIP memory one complete bank at a time. For SIMMs and SIPs, the problem is much easier. The circuit strip contains all the individual chips needed to add up to the rated capacity. But some SIMM systems require that at least two SIMM sockets be filled before any of the memory can be used.

To determine speed, look for a number following a hyphen. By adding one or two zeros to the number, you get the speed of a chip in nanoseconds. For example, a 1 or 10 means 100 nanoseconds (ns); a 12 means 120ns; an 8 means 80ns. The smaller the number, the faster the chip.

Some typical chip markings

4164-1
64K x 100ns
Single 64K chip (takes 9 to make full 64K) rated at 100ns

41256-7
256K x 70ns
Single 256K chip (takes 9 to make full 256K) rated at 70ns

4464-8
64K x 80ns
Single 64K chip (takes 8 to make full 64K) rated at 80ns

411000-6
1MB x 60ns
1MB chip (takes 9 to make full 1MB) rated at 60ns

HOT TIP Unfortunately, there is no standard way of marking chips for capacity and speed. The examples shown here will work in most situations, but it's always possible to find chips that defy deciphering. The lack of a hyphen, for example, may make it difficult to determine the speed of your memory. If all else fails, remove a DIP or SIMM, put it in a paper envelope to prevent damage from static, and take it to an electronics or computer supply dealer. Make it the dealer's problem. The dealer should have a catalog that gives the details hidden in a chip's part number.

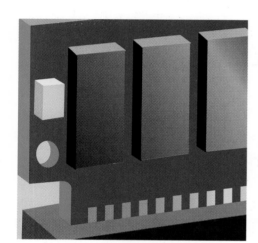

How to Identify Bad Memory Chips

HAVE A CONFESSION to make. The first time I had a memory chip go bad on me, I didn't fix it myself. I saw the message on my screen about a parity error and memory malfunctioning, and I panicked totally. This was my first PC. I'd had it only long enough for the warranty to expire, and I feared this was an omen of more bad news. Somehow, I imagined, if I got this fixed quickly, this electronic gangrene wouldn't spread to the rest of my PC.

I took my PC to a little computer repair shop. Twenty-four hours later, my PC was fixed and the bill was $70, of which, if I remember right, $5 was for the chip and the rest for labor.

Could I have done the repair myself? Yes, but only if I had known some of the tips and methods in this book—and if I hadn't gone into a state of high anxiety.

When a memory error is detected—most often when the memory is checked during boot-up—your PC will display a message that is supposed to identify the location of the faulty chip. But interpreting the message is daunting because the messages are universally cryptic. They may involve a number in *hexadecimal*—a 16-base number system that uses *A, B, C, D, E,* and *F* to supplement the *0* to *9* that make up the 10-base decimal number system. And you might have to get into some binary math—base-2. If your PC is still functioning after the memory error and you have Windows, the Windows calculator is a handy way to translate numbers among the three systems.

You should also remember that the error messages are reporting the byte in RAM at which a memory error is discovered. How this translates into a physical location depends on the size of the memory chips and whether there are any memory-expansion boards.

What I can do here is tell you the procedures to follow that will take care of the most common memory troubleshooting for older PCs that have DIP RAM chips and memory-expansion boards and for newer PCs that have all of their memory in SIMMs. (The same applies to SIPs, but SIPs turn up so much less frequently that, from now on, I'm simply going to refer to SIMMs. If you have SIPs—and you should know who you are by now—please do a little on-the-fly mental translation.) SIMM troubleshooting is much simpler because you usually don't have to figure RAM expansion cards into the process as you do with older PCs.

Because of a lack of uniformity in configuring memory and reporting when RAM is on the fritz, your situation may not fall into the circumstances I'm going to describe. The IBM PS/2 computers, for example, have their own, specialized memory error messages. You should check the manual that came with your PC to find out what it has to say about memory errors and how to interpret error messages. Between your manual and this book, you have a good chance of figuring out what to do. But if you can't, or if all this business about memory is simply beginning to sound terribly disheartening, you can always take your PC to a repair shop. It's nothing to be ashamed of. It's something all of us, *ah-hem,* do from time to time—when we've reached the limits of our expertise. But in any case, check out this chapter. It has some emergency tricks that could save you if a memory problem arises at a time when or place where you can't get professional help.

Translating DIP Memory Error Codes (PC/XT and AT-class PCs)

Locating the RAM Bank with a Bad Memory Chip

1 The monitor displays an error code that includes a number in hexadecimal. The first two digits identify the bank where the faulty chip is located.

2 Multiply the first two digits by 4 if the computer is an XT or earlier-class PC, or by 64 if the computer is an AT-class PC. An AT is used as an example here.

3 Check your memory chips to determine their capacity. (See Chapter 5 for details.) And divide the results of multiplying the first two numbers by the size of your memory chips, which is the amount of memory contained in each bank. Disregard any remainders. The result is the number of the bank that contains the bad chip. Check your manual or look for a label to determine which is the first bank. The first bank is usually marked "BANK 0."(If you have more than one memory-expansion adapter installed, count the banks starting with the first bank on the first adapter.)

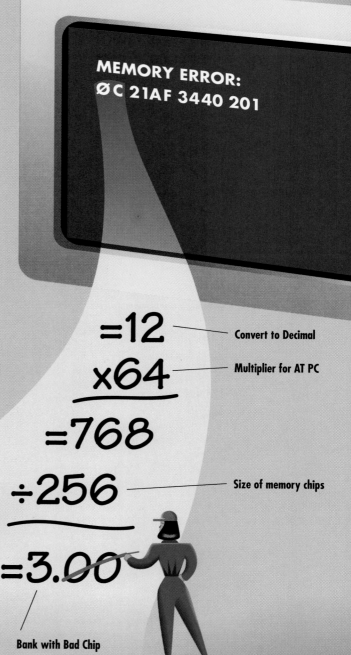

MEMORY ERROR:
Ø C 21AF 3440 201

=12 — Convert to Decimal

x64 — Multiplier for AT PC

=768

÷256 — Size of memory chips

=3.00

Bank with Bad Chip

Locating the Bad Memory Chip within a Bank

1 Some error messages may read "parity check 1" or "parity check 2"; 1 means a bad chip on the motherboard; 2 means a bad chip on an expansion board. If the last numbers in the error message are *201*, they simply confirm that the error is in the RAM area. For an XT or earlier computer, convert the last two hexadecimal digits before the *201* into a binary number. For an AT-class PC, convert the last four digits before the *201* into a binary number.

MEMORY ERROR:
Ø C 21AF 3440 201

Convert to binary

01000000

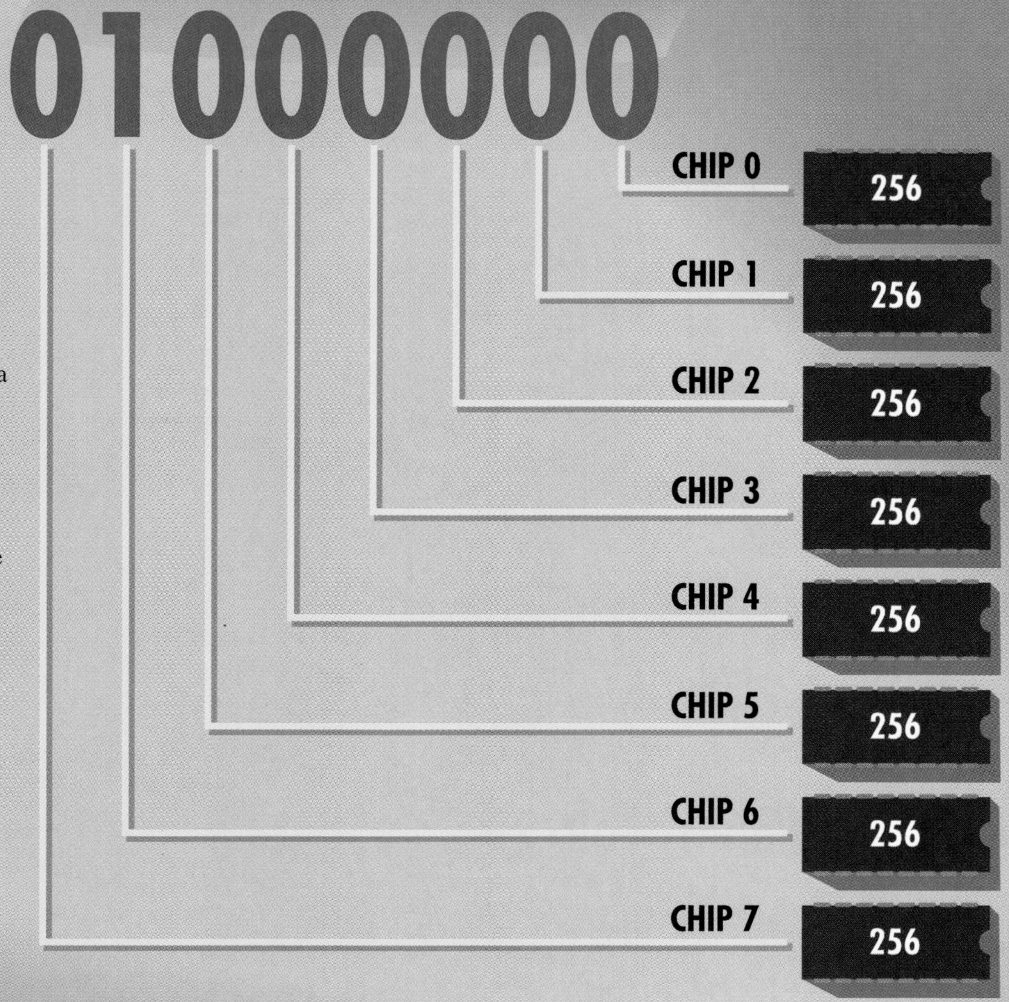

2 Each *1* in the binary number represents a failed RAM chip. Count from right to left, remembering that the first chip in a bank is numbered *0*, the second chip is numbered *1*, then *2*, etc. In our example, the bad chip should be *6*. Check your manual to determine which is the starting chip in a bank.

CHIP 0 — 256

CHIP 1 — 256

CHIP 2 — 256

CHIP 3 — 256

CHIP 4 — 256

CHIP 5 — 256

CHIP 6 — 256

CHIP 7 — 256

Translating DIP Memory Error Codes

Locating a Faulty SIMM Memory Module

1 When a PC with SIMM memory boots, a flaw in one of the SIMMs causes the computer to ignore all memory past the flawed chip so that it reports less memory installed than there actually is. The amount of RAM that the PC reports it has is the clue to the location of the bad module. In the example here, the computer has 4 megabytes of memory provided by four 1MB SIMMs, but the boot-up reports that there is only 1792K installed.

ROM BIOS (C)1990 AMI
1792 KB OK

2 Because a 384K section of RAM called the upper-memory block is not counted until all other memory is accounted for, add 384K to the amount of total RAM reported erroneously by the boot-up message. Divide that number by the amount of the RAM capacity of each SIMM module. (See Chapter 5.) In our example, we have 1MB (1024K) SIMMs that, when divided into the amount of memory reported as OK during boot-up, yields 2.125. That means the memory was all OK through the second SIMM (2048K). The bad memory must lie in the third SIMM.

$$
\begin{array}{r}
1792 \\
+384 \\
\hline
=2176 \text{ K} \\
\div 1024 \\
\hline
=2.125
\end{array}
$$

SIMM 4
4096K

SIMM 3
3072K

SIMM 2
2048K

SIMM 1
1024K

HOT TIP If you can't replace a faulty SIMM immediately, you can still keep working if you swap the faulty SIMM with the last SIMM on the motherboard. That minimizes the chance of your software having to access that memory, causing an error. If a faulty chip-error message drives you nuts while you're still using the chip, turn off the error detection in your CMOS setup.

3 Check your manual or look for a printed label on the circuit board that tells which SIMM is the first. If the manual does not tell you, you can assume that the first module with its DIP chips facing out is the first SIMM. Count from it to locate the faulty module. Because you cannot replace the individual RAM chip on the SIMM that is ailing, you'll have to replace the entire SIMM. (See Chapter 7 on installing memory.)

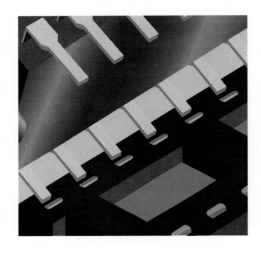

How to Replace or Add Memory

THE BEST THING you can do for you and your PC is to add more memory to it. It is almost impossible to add so much memory that your programs say, "Sorry, no thanks. We've had enough." Software is insatiably hungry for memory—particularly if your system is running Windows, Windows NT, or OS/2. Adding more memory will make your software run faster. You'll get greater convenience in multitasking environments because you'll be able to switch from one program to another instantly. And if you're running Windows, you'll be less likely to have application errors that crash your system.

And compared with such horrors as installing a sound card or programming a VCR, installing memory is one of the easiest things you can do. You can double the amount of RAM in 15 to 30 minutes.

Before adding memory, be sure to review Chapter 5 and determine what type of memory you already have and how much room there is for more chips. If you have an AT or earlier PC that uses DIP chips, and all the sockets for them on the motherboard are already full, then you may have to buy a memory expansion board to get any more RAM into your machine. Actually, in a situation like that, you should buy a new PC before wasting money upgrading a PC that's likely to have a seriously outdated processor, memory cache, video controller, and other components, which are just as crucial as memory to the performance of your PC. But assuming you've still got some open DIP sockets on the motherboard or on a memory expansion board that's already installed, you'll find out in this chapter how to install more memory. You'll also find out how to remove any bad chips using the techniques in Chapter 6, and how to replace the chips with good ones.

If you have a PC with SIMM or SIP memory, when you check under the hood, you may find that all the SIMM sockets are taken up. This doesn't necessarily mean you can't increase the size of your PC's RAM. And if you do find some empty sockets, it doesn't mean you can put just any SIMMs into the empty spots.

Usually all the SIMM sockets must have the same capacity SIMMs installed in them. Except with a few rare motherboards, if you only have two of four SIMM sockets filled, each with a 1MB SIMM, you can't add two 4MB SIMMs to the empty sockets to get 10MB of RAM. You must either fill the two empty sockets with 1MB SIMMs or you must remove the two 1MB SIMMs already installed before you add SIMMs with a different capacity. If all four sockets are taken up with 1MB modules for a total of 4MB, you can remove all of them and install two 4MB SIMMs for 8MB of RAM, leaving you room to upgrade later to 16MB by filling the two remaining sockets with additional 4MB SIMMs.

Before you run off to buy any SIMM chips, however, check your PC's manual to find out the maximum amount of RAM that it will handle. Most will handle at least 32MB, which is more than you really need, for now anyway. Get the most RAM that your machine and your budget can handle.

Adding memory is generally one of the least expensive things you can do to improve the performance of your PC. The prices of memory vary depending on supply and demand and the U.S. trade conditions with the Pacific Rim countries. But typically, you can buy 1 megabyte of memory in SIMM format for anywhere from $40 to $90. DIP memory prices run a bit less than that.

Don't waste your money on brand names or faster memory. I've never heard anyone claim that one brand of memory chips is better than any other, although experienced repair people note that RAM chips made in Korea may run hotter than chips from Japan, increasing the likelihood of failure. Otherwise, buy the least expensive. And don't buy chips that are faster than the ones you already have in your system. The faster chips will work OK, but you won't see any improvement in performance. Your PC is designed to work with memory at a certain speed. It simply doesn't care if the chips you install are faster.

On the other hand, don't buy chips slower than the ones you already have installed. They're cheaper, but they will interfere with the performance of your system. Ideally, buy DIPs or SIMMs, the speed of which matches the memory that came with your system. If you can't find RAM the same speed as you already have, and you don't mind paying for a capability your system can't use, then buy faster memory.

Once you have your new memory, set aside some time so that you can do the installation at leisure, take the safety and antistatic precautions described in the first part of this book, and then follow the instructions on the upcoming pages.

DIP Chip RAM

Removing DIP Chips

1 Making sure you've grounded yourself, place each prong of a chip extractor on either of the narrow ends of a DIP chip. It's not always easy to get the bent tips under the chip. You may have to wiggle the extractor a bit.

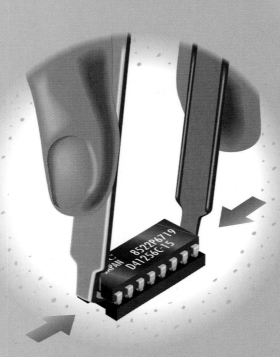

2 Squeeze both of the prongs of the extractor together.

3 Rock the extractor back and forth in the long direction of the chip until the chip comes free.

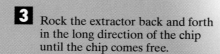
HOT TIP If you don't have a chip extractor, you can use a small flat-head screwdriver to pry up on the RAM chip, alternating between the two ends until the chip is loose enough to pull free.

Inserting DIP Chips

1 DIP chips often come with their pins bent out slightly. This makes them difficult to insert. Before trying to insert a DIP RAM chip into a socket, first put the chip on a hard surface, such as a desktop, so that the chip is on its side. Gently press down on the chip so that the pins are bent in until they form a 90-degree angle with the body of the chip.

2 Locate a notch on one end of the chip, and find a similar notch on the socket or in a printed outline of the socket on the motherboard. You must insert the chip so that the notches on it and on the socket are pointed in the same direction.

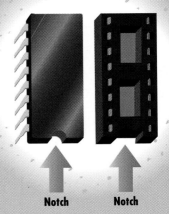

Notch   **Notch**

3 Insert one side of the chip into the socket first. Place it so that the tips of all the pins are barely in the holes. Inspect it carefully from both sides to make sure none of the pins are outside their holes.

4 Lower the other side of the chip so that its pins go slightly into their holes. You may have to press sideways slightly toward the side that's already in the socket to make the pins on the opposite side fit properly.

5 Stop and inspect the chip from all sides. You want to make sure that when you press the chip in, none of the pins will be bent under the chip or outside the socket.

6 When you're sure all the chips are lined up, press evenly along the length of the chip. It should go all the way into the socket so that you see no space between the chip and the socket.

7 After the memory is installed, you may need to let your PC know it has new memory. On older systems, how this is done varies. Check your PC's manual for the correct settings. On more recent systems, make the change in the CMOS settings.

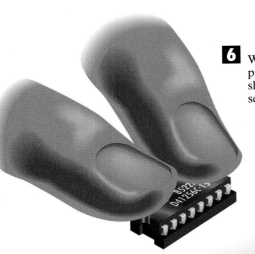

HOT TIP If you do bend a pin under a RAM chip when you try to insert it, remove the chip and use needle-nose pliers to straighten it. As long as you don't bend the pin back and forth too much, it should hold up for at least one more try.

SIMMs

Removing SIMMs

1 Making sure you've grounded yourself, use tweezers or a small flat-head screwdriver on one end of the SIMM to bend back slightly a plastic or metal tab that locks that end of the SIMM in place. Pull the SIMM forward slightly so that it doesn't get locked back again, and then do the same for the tab on the other end of the SIMM.

2 Tilt the SIMM away from two small prongs that fit into holes in the SIMM. Lift it out of the socket and remember the direction the small chips on the SIMM were facing before you removed them.

HOT TIP If the tabs holding in the SIMM are plastic, exerting too much pressure against them can break them off. If that happens, you don't have to run out and buy a new motherboard. The SIMMs fit snugly even without both tabs. Continue to use your PC normally and if you then experience memory problems traced to that SIMM, reseating it periodically may save you the hassle and expense of replacing an entire circuit board.

Installing SIMMs

1 If you're installing all new SIMMs, remember the direction the small chips on the SIMMs were facing before you took them out. You'll want the new SIMMs to face the same way. If you've forgotten already, notice that there is a notch on one end of the SIMM, and a notch in the bottom middle of the SIMM. Together these notches prevent you from inserting a SIMM in the wrong direction.

Notch   Notch

2 Insert the SIMM at an angle as far as it will go into the socket.

3 Press the SIMM into place until the tabs lock around both ends of the SIMM. On some sockets, the tabs will snap into place easily. Other tabs require that you pull them out slightly so you can push the SIMM into place. A third hand is helpful in this situation. If you don't have one, work on first one end of the SIMM and then the other.

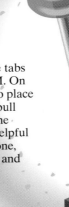

4 Press the SIMM forward until the two prongs stick into the holes in the SIMM. If the SIMM isn't at a 90-degree angle to the motherboard, that's OK. Some SIMM sockets are designed so that the SIMMs stick straight up; others leave the SIMMs leaning in unison.

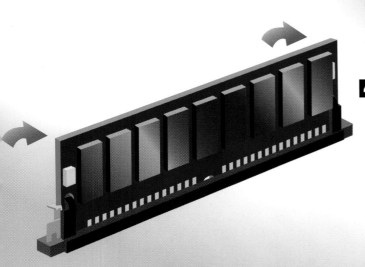

5 After the memory is installed, change your CMOS settings, if needed, to let your PC know how much memory it now has.

EXPANSION BOARDS

CONTENTS

WE SHOULD ALL thank the creators of the original IBM PC for not being egotists. They didn't have the arrogance to believe that there was no room to improve on the personal computer they had designed. In fact, the design was an open invitation for others to create products that would improve—expand—the capabilities of the PC. The design provided several unused connectors called, appropriately enough, *expansion slots*. Others could design expansion cards or adapters that would plug into the slots to provide new hardware capabilities.

The expansion slots work through the PC's expansion *bus*—the common denominator of the personal computer. No matter what type of processor, hard drives, video cards, mouse, or any other component that your PC may use, they all must communicate with each other. And they do so through the bus. You can't really point to one component and call it the bus: A large portion of the bus consists of the hair-fine circuitry printed on the motherboard, some of the bus consists of the microchips on the motherboard, and another big chunk is made up of the expansion slots.

There are six kinds of expansion slots that you might find in a personal computer. They represent the improvements that have been made over the years in a PC's communication with its components—mostly in the speed with which adapter cards can shuttle data back and forth between the CPU and the components attached through the slots. But even the earliest of the slots—the one found in the original IBM PC/XT, which could send data only 8 bits at a time—is still found in some recent PCs. That's because the 8-bit PC/XT slot is inexpensive to create, and some adapter cards, such as a serial port or mouse card, are, by nature, so slow that the newer, faster adapter cards are overkill.

The most common type of slot is the *ISA*, which stands for *Industry Standard Architecture*. This is a 16-bit slot that made its first appearance on the IBM-AT. You'll sometimes find it referred to as an AT slot. The fact that it has not been completely replaced by later technology is a tribute to just how effective the ISA slot is and to the fact there are more ISA adapters manufactured than any other kind.

The ISA slot is, however, limited to handling data 16 bits at a time, which was acceptable with the Intel 80286 microprocessor that came on the IBM-AT. But today's processors can handle up to 64 bits of data at a time, and several later expansion bus designs have been created to let the bus keep up with the rest of the system. IBM first introduced the *Micro Channel Architecture*, or *MCA*, to provide a way to handle 32 bits of data at a time. For a while, IBM tried to keep the MCA architecture proprietary, so that other companies would have to pay IBM for the right to use MCA technology. But other manufacturers, used to the open architecture of the IBM PCs, didn't jump on the bandwagon. The result is that there was no mass demand for MCA adapters, and expansion-board companies continued to concentrate on the more popular ISA cards. Further, you couldn't use the older ISA cards in the new MCA slots. For a peripheral such as a modem or scanner that can't really benefit from 32-bit data transmission, MCA was an expense with no benefit. Several computer companies tried to counter MCA with a standard of their own, *Extended Industry Standard Architecture*, or *EISA*. EISA expansion slots accept both specially created 32-bit EISA cards or the older ISA cards.

In addition to 32-bit data transfers, the MCA and EISA designs provided intelligent ways to install the cards, eliminating having to set the minuscule switches that are common on ISA cards. But after several years, neither MCA or EISA architecture has had a serious impact on computing. Until recently, most PCs were sold with a combination of ISA 16-bit and PC/XT 8-bit slots.

Beginning in 1992, however, a new slot design came along that did have an impact—the *local bus*. The name derives from the fact that ISA buses are limited to moving data about on the circuity designed for the original AT bus at the clock speed of the AT computer that originated ISA. That speed is only about 6 MHz. Since the time of the AT, however, processors that work at 25MHz, 33MHz, or more have become common. These processors communicate at their full speed with RAM on what's called a local bus because it's not a bus for the entire PC, but serves only a small, local area of the motherboard. The first local bus—the *VESA local bus*—was created by a committee called Video Electronics Standards Association (VESA). VESA was looking for a way to combat the slowness inherent with hard drives and the Windows graphical environment. The graphical environment of Windows requires that much more data be sent to the video adapter, and more disk thrashing occurs than is necessary with simple DOS-based software. The solution VESA came up with was to tap into the local bus, which was usually traveled only by the processor and RAM. Speed-starved Windows users could see the benefit instantly, and the VL was an immediate success, not only because it made Windows faster but because it is a relatively cheap and simple modification to ISA boards. Local bus has also proved beneficial when used with adapters that control drives; those adapters also need to shuttle large amounts of data quickly between the drives and memory.

Since VESA introduced its solution, several computer manufacturers, led by micro-processor manufacturer Intel Corp., have come up with another version of a local bus, the *Peripheral Component Interconnect* or *PCI local bus*. The PCI bus is designed to allow faster data transfers than even the VL-bus does. The two technologies are currently shar-ing the claim to be a standard. Eventually, one of them may claim sole victory (or they could both lose out to something even better). For now, though, VL-bus is being seen more often on inexpensive PCs. and PCI is cropping up on computers where ultimate performance is worth a bigger price tag.

There is one more term related to expansion slots you should be familiar with: *plug and play*. Of course, computer components are rarely like that, which is why you're read-ing this book. But Intel, Microsoft, and other major computer companies are working on what they call a plug-and-play design for adapter cards and other components. These adapter cards would carry information on a chip that identifies them and what type of memory and communications resources they need to work. A special BIOS in plug-and-play PCs would read that information and sort out a solution for all the requests for resources without your intervention.

PART THREE

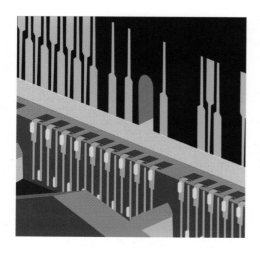

CHAPTER

8

Identifying the Expansion Slot

YOU CAN ALMOST predict what type of expansion slot you have in your PC if you know the year in which it was made. The first PCs, which debuted in 1981, had only 8-bit PC/XT expansion slots. It wasn't until 1984, when the IBM-AT first appeared, that we got the 16-bit slots that eventually came to be called the ISA bus.

From then until now, just about any non-IBM PC you bought was going to have mostly ISA slots. If you bought an IBM-PC for several years after 1987, it would have only MCA expansion slots. But even IBM implicitly has admitted MCA was not a big winner when, after a few years, it began selling ISA machines again, although it didn't drop MCA PCs entirely.

Rival EISA has not been significantly more successful than MCA. It has appeared most often on PCs that act as file servers on networks—a situation that requires the speediest transfer of files possible.

If you bought your PC anytime after 1992, without opening it up or looking at the brand name, I'd be willing to bet that it has one or two local-bus slots—maybe PCI but more likely a VL-bus—maybe one PC/XT 8-bit slot and the rest 16-bit ISA slots.

If you have a PC/XT slot, try to use it for components that are naturally slow, such as the parallel and serial ports or for a scanner adapter. An ISA adapter slot is your everyday workhorse, good for a sound card, CD-ROM drive controller, or most hard drive controllers. A local bus slot should be used with a local bus adapter for video and, if you have a second local bus slot, for a drive controller.

Remember that to take full advantage of any type of expansion slot, you must have an adapter card made for that specific type of slot. You can put an 8-bit card into an ISA slot, but you only get 8-bit performance out of it. You can put an ISA card into an EISA slot, but you only get ISA performance out of it.

Finally, if you can't find an adapter for, say, the video or drive controller, check your PC's manual. Some PCs have motherboards with these controllers built into them, instead of having slots and separate adapter cards. That's no problem, unless you want to install newer or faster versions of those adapters. In that case, your manual should tell you how you can disable the built-in adapters.

Which Are Your Expansion Slots?

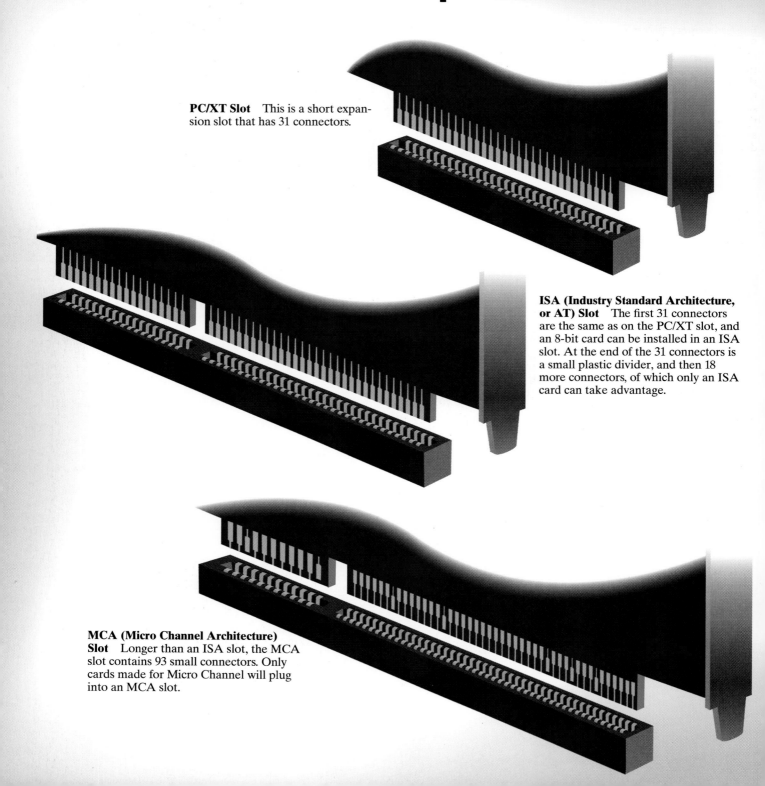

PC/XT Slot This is a short expansion slot that has 31 connectors.

ISA (Industry Standard Architecture, or AT) Slot The first 31 connectors are the same as on the PC/XT slot, and an 8-bit card can be installed in an ISA slot. At the end of the 31 connectors is a small plastic divider, and then 18 more connectors, of which only an ISA card can take advantage.

MCA (Micro Channel Architecture) Slot Longer than an ISA slot, the MCA slot contains 93 small connectors. Only cards made for Micro Channel will plug into an MCA slot.

EISA (Extended Industry Architecture) Slot   The EISA slot accepts both PX/XT and ISA adapter cards. Plastic tabs allow the older-style cards to slide into an EISA slot only far enough to reach pins that are the equivalent of pins in an ISA expansion slot. But an EISA card can enter farther into the slot and come in contact with an additional row of connectors, roughly doubling the number of connections.

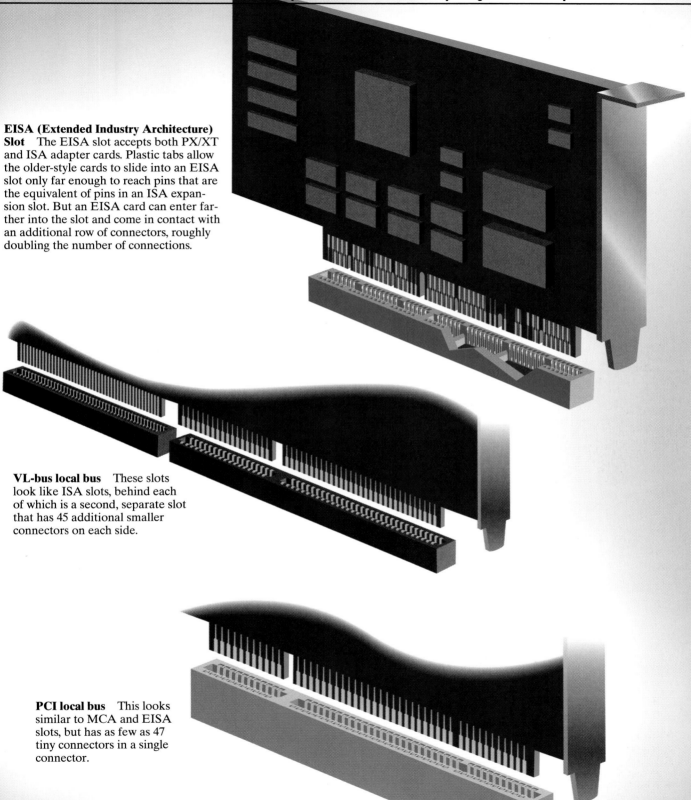

VL-bus local bus   These slots look like ISA slots, behind each of which is a second, separate slot that has 45 additional smaller connectors on each side.

PCI local bus   This looks similar to MCA and EISA slots, but has as few as 47 tiny connectors in a single connector.

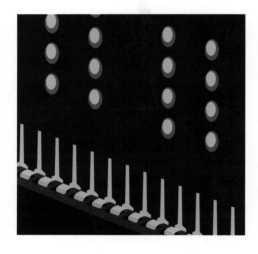

Installing an Expansion Card

OF ALL THE PC components you can work with, expansion cards are the most scary. Maybe it's because they're so crammed with chips, and resistors, and other strange-looking electrical gizmos. Maybe it's because a new expansion card represents such a major change in your PC.

Whatever the cause of your trepidation about working with expansion, or adapter, cards, the truth is that inserting the card is one of the simpler jobs you can do on your computer. On the other hand, getting the card to work cooperatively with the rest of your hardware can be frustrating, and we'll confront that in the next chapter. But to get an adapter board in or out of your PC requires nothing more than a screwdriver or nut driver, both hands, a bit of patience, and perhaps a flashlight.

The only serious difficulty in working with expansion boards is that everything is made to fit tightly. That means you have to be careful about the exact angle of a board as you try to insert it. And there's a trick to working with the little metal bracket on all expansion cards that I'll show you in the next few pages.

A general rule about working with PCs is particularly relevant here: Don't be afraid of pressing and pushing parts firmly to make them fit, but don't overdo it. How much is overdoing it? After a while, you will be able to tell the difference between the amount of natural resistance that's appropriate from tightly fitting components and the resistance you get when trying to insert a component someplace it just wasn't meant to go. The best gauge I can think of is this: If you're sweating, grunting, or trembling, you're trying too hard. It's time to back off and try to figure out what's being more stubborn than you are.

If you have got the right board for the slot, if it's positioned properly, and if nearby cables aren't dangling in the way, a child can slip a board into an expansion slot. We'll start with a simpler task—removing a card—that you may need to do before installing a replacement. Then we'll graduate to installing an adapter card.

Removing an Expansion Card

1 After taking the usual precautions of disconnecting the power cord and grounding yourself, open the case. Use a screwdriver or nut driver to undo the machine screw that fastens the expansion-card bracket to the back of your PC. Tape the screw to the computer's case so it doesn't get lost.

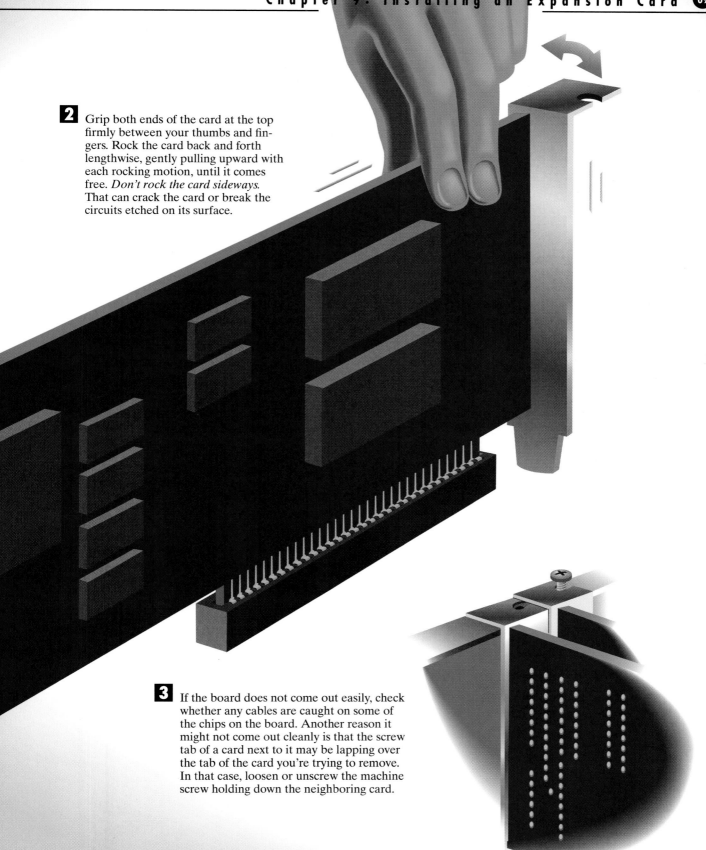

2 Grip both ends of the card at the top firmly between your thumbs and fingers. Rock the card back and forth lengthwise, gently pulling upward with each rocking motion, until it comes free. *Don't rock the card sideways.* That can crack the card or break the circuits etched on its surface.

3 If the board does not come out easily, check whether any cables are caught on some of the chips on the board. Another reason it might not come out cleanly is that the screw tab of a card next to it may be lapping over the tab of the card you're trying to remove. In that case, loosen or unscrew the machine screw holding down the neighboring card.

Inserting an Expansion Card

1 After disconnecting the power cord and grounding yourself, open the case and look for an unused expansion slot that, if possible, doesn't have expansion cards installed on either side of it. The less cramped the card is, the easier it will be to work with it. If you can't find a slot that has empty slots on both sides, settle for one with an empty slot on one side. Be sure to choose a slot that matches the type of card you're trying to install—ISA, EISA, MCA, or local bus (see Chapter 8).

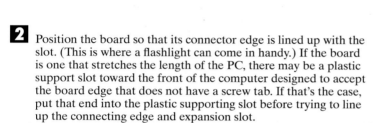

2 Position the board so that its connector edge is lined up with the slot. (This is where a flashlight can come in handy.) If the board is one that stretches the length of the PC, there may be a plastic support slot toward the front of the computer designed to accept the board edge that does not have a screw tab. If that's the case, put that end into the plastic supporting slot before trying to line up the connecting edge and expansion slot.

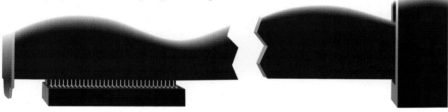

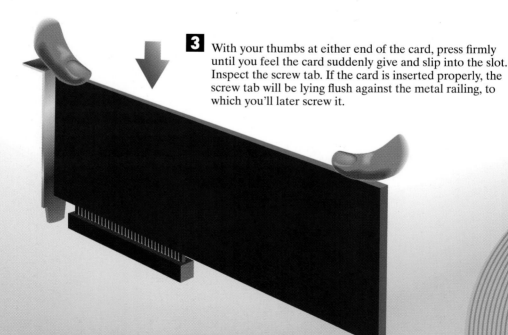

3 With your thumbs at either end of the card, press firmly until you feel the card suddenly give and slip into the slot. Inspect the screw tab. If the card is inserted properly, the screw tab will be lying flush against the metal railing, to which you'll later screw it.

4 If the card will not go into the slot or if the screw tab doesn't rest flat against the railing, the most likely problem is a second metal tab at the bottom of the card. Remove the card and using your fingers, bend the tab out slightly. You don't have to bend it much. In fact, you may not even be able to see a difference, but the slight bend is all it needs. Try reinserting the card, and if it still won't work, bend the tab in the opposite direction.

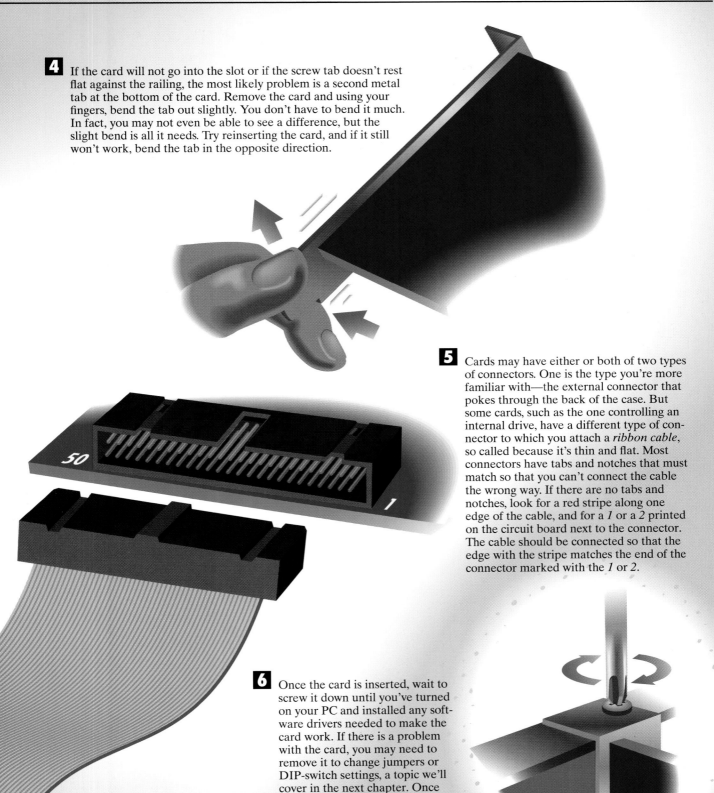

5 Cards may have either or both of two types of connectors. One is the type you're more familiar with—the external connector that pokes through the back of the case. But some cards, such as the one controlling an internal drive, have a different type of connector to which you attach a *ribbon cable*, so called because it's thin and flat. Most connectors have tabs and notches that must match so that you can't connect the cable the wrong way. If there are no tabs and notches, look for a red stripe along one edge of the cable, and for a *1* or a *2* printed on the circuit board next to the connector. The cable should be connected so that the edge with the stripe matches the end of the connector marked with the *1* or *2*.

6 Once the card is inserted, wait to screw it down until you've turned on your PC and installed any software drivers needed to make the card work. If there is a problem with the card, you may need to remove it to change jumpers or DIP-switch settings, a topic we'll cover in the next chapter. Once you're satisfied it's working properly, turn off your PC, screw down the card, and replace the cover.

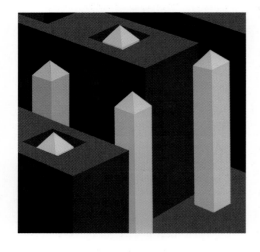

Making Expansion Cards Work Together

SO YOU FOLLOWED the instructions in the previous chapter and installed a new expansion board. But when you try to use the new feature that the expansion board is supposed to provide—a CD-ROM drive, a fax, or a scanner—it doesn't work. Or it works, but something else doesn't. Or maybe your whole PC doesn't work. What you've got is a case of *resource conflict*. The good news is that resource conflict isn't fatal. The chances are excellent that you can pull all parts of your computer through this so that each is working exactly as it's supposed to work. The bad news is that it can be a tedious process, and you may have to resort to calling tech support for at least one of your expansion boards. But take a deep breath, and with any luck, we'll have your PC back on its feet in less than an hour.

It will help if you understand the resources that are at the base of the conflict. There are four types of resources: *interrupt request lines* (IRQs); *direct-memory-access channels* (DMAs); *upper memory blocks* (UMBs); and *input/output* (I/O) *addresses*.

The interrupt request line is used by a device when it wants the attention of the processor. The device sends a signal along one line that's been assigned to it out of the 15 IRQs in the PC (only 7 IRQs in the IBM-XT–class machines). The signal is received by one of two chips called the *interrupt controllers*, which notify the microprocessor that it needs to interrupt whatever it's doing to handle a request from the device. If more than one device sends an interrupt signal at the same time, the interrupt controller decides which device gets priority. But if two devices try to send an interrupt on the same line, the interrupt controller can't distinguish one device from another.

Direct-memory-access channels are used by devices so that they can send data directly to and receive data directly from RAM without going through the processor. This speeds up operations all around because the device doesn't have to wait on the processor, and the processor can concentrate on other tasks. If two devices try to use the same DMA channel, data may be written to the wrong location or a device may retrieve data meant for another device. There are 16 DMAs on AT-class and later computers. Of these, DMA 2 is used by the floppy-disk controller; DMA 4 is used by the DMA controller itself; and DMA 5 is used by the hard-disk controller. All others are available for use by expansion boards.

Upper-memory blocks are areas of memory between 640K and 1 megabyte that the devices use for their own RAM BIOSes or device drivers. Some terminate-and-stay-resident (TSR) programs that work in the background may also load some of their code into UMBs. UMBs are identified by their memory addresses, usually noted in hexadecimal numbers. If the memory address that a new expansion card is set up to use is already being used by something else, one device's code will override the other device's code, and the first device will find instructions at that address that make no sense to it.

Input/output addresses are the physical locations where devices can be found on the computer's bus—its main circuitry that connects all the devices together. These are used so that software and other devices know where to send signals to another device. If two devices use the same I/O address, one may receive signals meant for the other device.

Of the four types of resources, the three you should be most concerned with are IRQs, DMAs, and I/Os. If you're lucky, you can install expansion cards that don't use the same resources and you won't have any problems. But the more you load up your system, the more likely you are to run into a conflict. Luckily, most expansion cards can be set to use alternative IRQs, DMAs, and I/O addresses. You can sometimes even have two devices that use a common setting. The sound card in my PC, for example, uses IRQ 7, which is also used by the LPT1 parallel port that my printer is connected to. Since I never print anything at the same time that I run, say, a multimedia game full of laser gun sounds, the two can coexist.

For those with MCA or EISA personal computers, the conflict problems are minimized. Expansion cards for PCs with those types of buses can be configured through software utilities. Someday all this fuss with resources won't exist for all PCs. A new standard for buses and expansion cards, called Plug and Play, is being devised by Intel Corporation and Microsoft Corporation, the companies that produce most of the processors and operating systems in use today. With Plug and Play, the BIOS and operating system will get information stored on each card about the resources the cards can use, and they'll juggle the settings for each until they find a combination with no conflicts.

But tomorrow's not here yet. So let's assume your luck has run out. The new card you installed has created some kind of conflict. First, I'll give you a quick lesson in the types of switches—*dip switches* and *jumpers*—used to control what resources are used by a card. Different settings of a dip switch, for example, may tell an expansion card to use DMA 1 instead of DMA 3. Similarly, by changing a jumper, you may be able to tell a device to use a different I/O address. After we've looked at the switches, we'll cover the steps for resolving a conflict.

Expansion Cards

Dip Switches

Change the setting of a switch by pressing down on the high end with a pen, straightened paper clip, or any other object narrow enough to let you change one switch without changing the switches on either side. *Warning: don't use pencils.*

Dip switches are tiny rocker or slide switches grouped in a plastic housing.

Numbers identify each switch.

Some banks of dip switches clearly identify the on position and the off position. But not all dip switches are so conveniently marked. And the situation is complicated, because sometimes a feature is activated if you flip a dip switch to an off position. If you're not certain which way is on or off, compare the settings with those in the expansion card's manual. Often one of the switches is supposed to always be on or off. Use it to orient the on and off positions of the other switches.

Jumpers

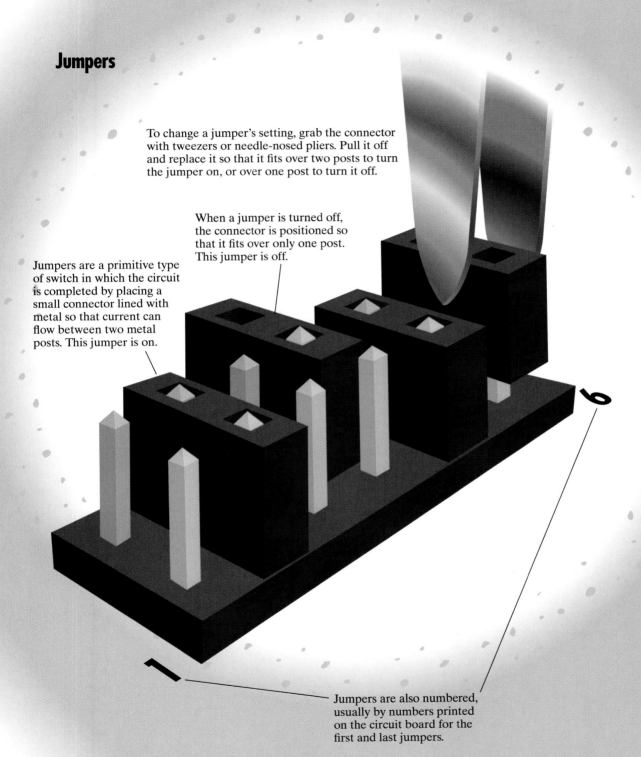

To change a jumper's setting, grab the connector with tweezers or needle-nosed pliers. Pull it off and replace it so that it fits over two posts to turn the jumper on, or over one post to turn it off.

When a jumper is turned off, the connector is positioned so that it fits over only one post. This jumper is off.

Jumpers are a primitive type of switch in which the circuit is completed by placing a small connector lined with metal so that current can flow between two metal posts. This jumper is on.

Jumpers are also numbered, usually by numbers printed on the circuit board for the first and last jumpers.

Troubleshooting Expansion Card Conflicts

If you have trouble determining the settings of any of your adapters, see the appendix, where there is a list of the most common expansion cards, and their IRQ, DMA, and UMB base memory addresses, along with the phone numbers of technical support for the companies that make the adapters. Consult the list to determine alternate settings you can use for your new or old cards.

File   Edit   Search   Options
————————————————————— CONFIG.SYS ——
REM **** Next line loads driver for Pro Audio sound ca
REM **** Settings are for DMA 5 and IRQ 7
REM DEVICE= C:\PROAUDIO\MVSOUND.SYS D:5 Q:7

1 For all the steps shown here, make sure that each time you install or remove an expansion card, you first shut down your PC, ground yourself by touching the metal housing of your PC, and then unplug it.

2 Remove the card you've just installed and disable any lines that its installation added to your CONFIG.SYS or AUTO-EXEC.BAT. Don't delete the lines. They are needed to tell the operating system what settings the card is using. Just type **REM** at the beginning of the lines. Later you can reenable the lines by removing REM—possibly after making changes to the command line's settings. Make sure that in the process of installing the new card, you didn't knock loose any cables or power connections. Plug in your PC, and make sure it's working properly without the new card.

Default Dip Switch Setting

OFF
1 2 3 4 5 6 7 8 9
ON

3 Inspect the card's dip switches or jumpers, checking the default settings on the new card against what its manual says they should be. Sometimes a card leaves the factory with the wrong settings. And sometimes the manual may be out of date. If the factory settings don't work, change the switches or jumpers to match the default settings shown in the manual, reinstall the card, and reboot your computer.

4 If your system still isn't working properly, it's time to find out what system resources the other expansion cards are using. Check your computer's manual and any manuals that came with other expansion cards that you've added to your PC. At this point, let's assume that you've installed all other expansion cards using their default settings. But if you know that you once installed another adapter card after changing its settings from their defaults, remove that card, if necessary, to determine what the settings are.

5 So that you don't have to go through this process each time you add an expansion board, keep a permanent record of your IRQs, DMAs, and UMB base memory addresses by filling in the form on the facing page. I've filled in the top line just to give you an example of the type of information to include. The far right column lists the types of devices that are generally associated with specific interrupts. [Continued on the next page.]

EXPANSION BOARD INVENTORY

IRQ	TYPICAL BASE ADDRESS	INTERNAL DEVICE	SLOT NUMBER	DEVICE OR ADAPTER INSTALLED	BASE ADDRESS USED BY DEVICE	DMA CHANNEL	TYPICAL DEVICE USING INTERRUPT
XT and AT SYSTEMS							
4	02F8	COM3	2	abc fax board	02F8	5	
NMI		NMI parity check					
0	0008	CMOS clock (Timer interrupt)					
1	0009	Keyboard					
2	000A	Interrupt controller (Cascade to IRQ9)					Network adapter, scanner, mouse
3	02F8 or 02E8	COM2 or COM 4					Mouse, fax modem, network adapter, scanner, tape drive, video
4	03F8 or 02F8	COM1 or COM3					Mouse, fax modem, CD-ROM, scanner
5	0278	LPT2 or hard disk					Sound card, mouse, fax modem, scanner, tape drive
6	035F0-03F7	Floppy disk controller					Tape drive
7	0278-027F	LPT1					Network adapter, scanner, mouse, sound card
AT SYSTEMS							
8	0070	Real-time clock					
9	0071	Cascade interrupt to IRQ2					SCSI adapter, scanner
10	0072	Available					Network adapter, SCSI adapter, mouse, sound card
11	0073	Available					Mouse, scanner, sound card, tape drive
12	0074	Available					SCSI adapter, mouse, scanner, video
13	0075	Math coprocessor					Mouse
14		Hard-disk controller					SCSI adapter, IDE adapter
15		Available					SCSI adapter, mouse

Troubleshooting Expansion Card Conflicts

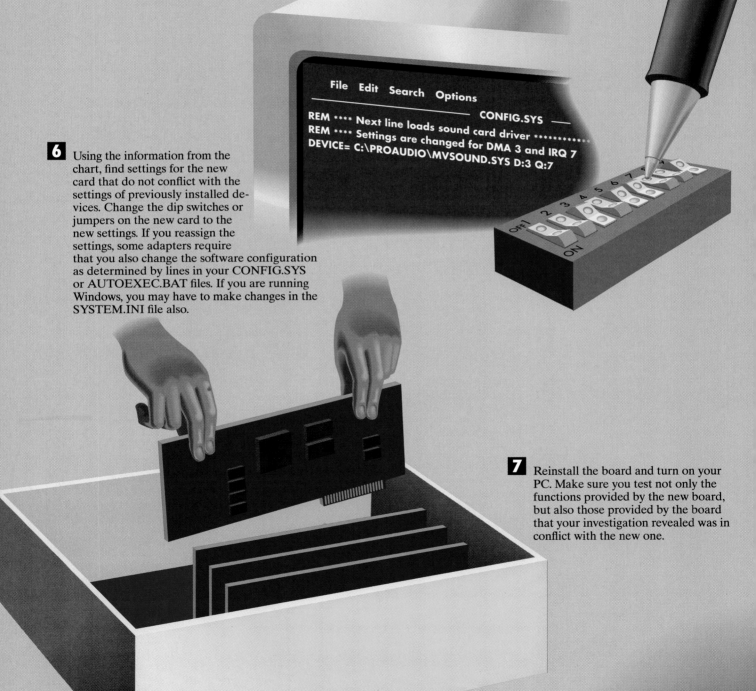

File   Edit   Search   Options

———— CONFIG.SYS ————
REM **** Next line loads sound card driver ***********
REM **** Settings are changed for DMA 3 and IRQ 7
DEVICE= C:\PROAUDIO\MVSOUND.SYS D:3 Q:7

6 Using the information from the chart, find settings for the new card that do not conflict with the settings of previously installed devices. Change the dip switches or jumpers on the new card to the new settings. If you reassign the settings, some adapters require that you also change the software configuration as determined by lines in your CONFIG.SYS or AUTOEXEC.BAT files. If you are running Windows, you may have to make changes in the SYSTEM.INI file also.

7 Reinstall the board and turn on your PC. Make sure you test not only the functions provided by the new board, but also those provided by the board that your investigation revealed was in conflict with the new one.

```
Microsoft Diagnostics version 2.00     11/22/94     9:04pm     Page 1
=======================================================================
---------------------------- IRQ Status ----------------------------
                                        Detected           Handled By
                                        --------           ----------
IRQ   Address     Description                              SYSCTRL.COM
---   -------     -----------            Yes               SYSCTRL.COM
 0    0BA7:115E   Timer Click            Yes               Default Handlers
 1    0BA7:1085   Keyboard               Yes               Default Handlers
 2    07A3:0057   Second 8259A           COM2:             Default Handlers
 3    07A3:006F   COM2: COM4:            COM1:             Default Handlers
 4    07A3:0087   COM1: COM3:            No                Default Handlers
 5    07A3:009F   LPT2:                                    $STACKS$
 6    07A3:00B7   Floppy Disk            Yes               Default Handlers
 7    058B:007C   LPT1:                  Yes               BIOS
 8    07A3:0052   Real-Time Clock        Yes               Default Handlers
 9    F000:F1A0   Redirected IRQ2        Yes               Default Handlers
10    07A3:00CF   (Reserved)                               Default Handlers
11    07A3:00E7   (Reserved)                               BIOS
12    07A3:00FF   (Reserved)                               Default Handlers
13    F000:F2E8   Math Coprocessor       Yes               Default Handlers
14    07A3:0117   Fixed Disk             Yes
15    07A3:012F   (Reserved)
```

Interrupt Information

8 If your system works, you're home free. Record the settings for the new card in the chart on the previous page. But if your system doesn't work properly, you can obtain information that may be helpful to solving the problem by running MSD.EXE, the diagnostic utility that comes with all recent versions of MS-DOS. To the left is a listing of the interrupt information for my computer. As you can see, under the Detected column, IRQ 5 is not being used by any device. And IRQs 10, 11, 12, and 15 are not in use but are reserved. I can probably assign a board to those interrupts also.

9 If you've tried all the alternative settings for your new expansion board—or if the board doesn't provide alternatives for some of the settings—change the settings on an older board that appears to be conflicting with it. Turn off your PC, ground yourself, unplug your computer, and pull out the old board, make a written notation of how it's already set, and then change its settings. Turn on your PC, and if it works, be sure to make a note of its new settings on the chart on the previous page.

10 If, at this point, the system still doesn't work, you have two alternatives: Redo the steps beginning with step 1 to make sure you noted accurately all jumper and dip swtich settings and UMB memory addresses, or admit defeat—at least temporarily. There's no shame to it. It's just time to call tech support. The tech-support specialists at the company that made your board are often aware of common conflicts as well as esoteric conditions that can prevent it from working. Have handy the information you entered on the previous chart. This will make it easier and faster for you and the technician to troubleshoot the problem. You can find tech support numbers for major companies in the Appendix.

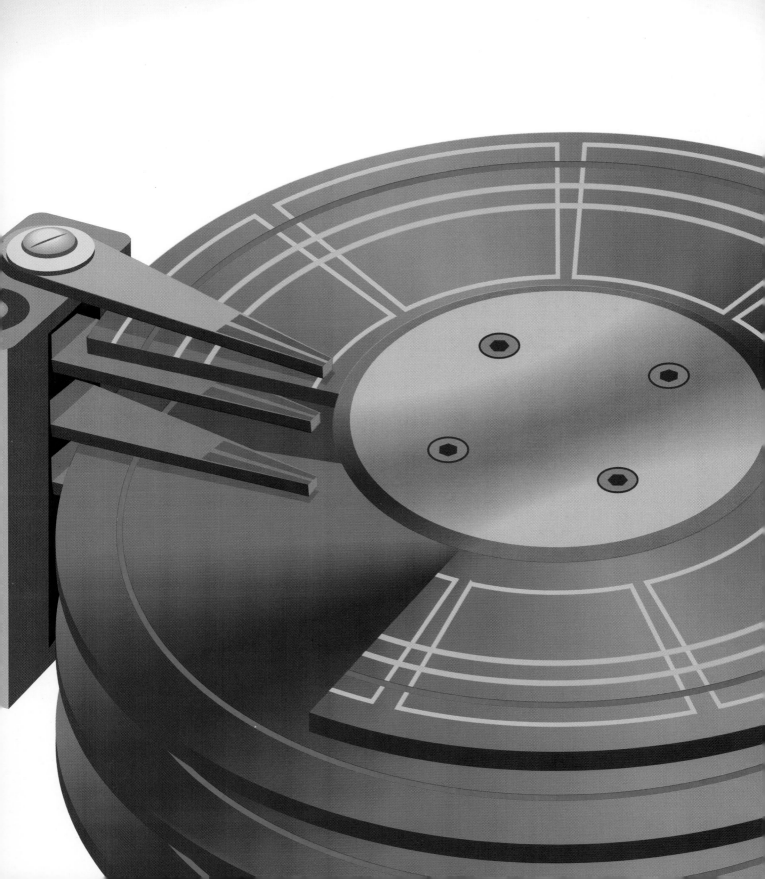

STORAGE DEVICES

4

C O N T E N T S

OVERVIEW

THIS IS WHERE it starts to be fun. Installing a new drive is the second best thing you can do to improve the capabilities of your personal computer. The first best thing for a PC running Windows is to add more memory, but the benefits are not as obvious. Sure, it seems like your word processor may be running a little faster, but it's not as apparent as displaying a directory and finding—another 200 megabytes of storage space!

At some point, you will have enough memory. After 16 megabytes of RAM, the advantages of adding more memory fall off until, at some point, you can't tell the difference if you throw another 4 megabytes of SIMMs into your machine. But you will never have enough storage space.

My first PC had no hard drives at all. And for a couple of years I was perfectly happy inserting a different floppy for each program I wanted to run. I was happy simply because hard drives were not an alternative. Then came the IBM-XT, complete with a 10MB hard drive, and I was on a never-ending uphill run for more and more memory. As soon as I could afford it, I bought a 10MB hard drive. Within a week, I was back at the computer dealer, trading it in on a 20MB drive. Within months I was back buying a second 20MB drive and a special kind of disk controller that could increase the capacity of both drives by 50 percent. Never mind that I'd heard such controllers were flaky. I had to have more storage space!

The 60MB of drive space did last me for several years, but of course today, that much space would be totally inadequate. The word processor that I use, WordPerfect 6.0 for Windows, takes up 28MB of storage by itself. Now I have more than a gigabyte of storage—1,000MB—and periodically, I still run out of room and have to search for files that I can delete.

Today's Windows programs use enormous amounts of drive space, which is reason enough to add another hard drive to your system. And the bigger your hard drive(s), the more you should consider adding another form of storage—a tape backup drive. In the old days when I had 60 megabytes of storage, I could spend a couple of hours feeding floppies into my PC to back up the hard drives. Today, that's just not practical. As your hard drive storage grows, so does your need for a tape drive. It's not a matter of if your hard drive will crash, it's a matter of when.

In this section, we'll look at what it takes to install an internal drive. As an example, we'll use a hard drive, but the same principles apply to a floppy drive, a tape drive, or a CD-ROM drive. You'll find that installation is not at all hard to do. Like I said, this is where it's fun.

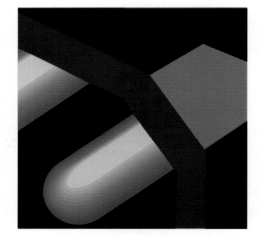

CHAPTER 11

Installing a Drive

THERE ARE SO many storage options today that it's not impossible to find a single PC that has a half-dozen types of storage drives attached to it. Every modern PC has at least two drives—a floppy drive and a hard, or fixed, drive. But you should be aware of the other storage options, because each of them has a good reason for being; each solves a different storage problem.

Here are the common types of drives you're likely to encounter and why you'd want to add one to your system.

5¼-inch Floppy Drive   This was the drive that the PC revolution began with. Although the capacity of the drive has increased over the years from 180K to 360K to 1.2MB, it's lost ground to the more convenient, hard-cased 3½-inch floppy. The main reason for having a 5¼-inch drive today is if you have a brother-in-law with an old XT and you have to swap files occasionally.

3½-inch Floppy Drive   The medium of choice for distributing programs and making portable copies of your data, this drive's maximum capacity can go as high as 2.88MB. This drive allows almost universal transfer of files, even with laptops, although it does exclude ancient PCs.

Hard Drive   This is the workhorse of the PC. Constantly spinning, it makes possible the quick access to the gargantuan numbers of files required by today's feature-rich, graphic-based programs. Someday we'll be telling youngsters how we once computed without them, the same way our grandparents told us how they didn't have cars or buses to get to schools that were five miles away.

There are several types of hard drives available today. The *form factor*—computer jargon for size and shape—is the most obvious difference. Some of the bigger drives—1 gigabyte or bigger—are still *full-height*, meaning that they fill a full-height drive bay that's a little under 3½ inches tall. Half-height drives fit into the same half-height drive bay that floppy drives fit into. (Once, children, floppy drives were full-height.) Half-heights are about 1¾ inches tall. The latest form factor is the quarter-height or 3½-inch hard drive, which is only 1-inch thick and about the size of a paperback. There are smaller drives, designed primarily for portable computers, but one of these sizes is the type you're mostly likely to install in your desktop or tower personal computer.

A more important consideration than form factors is the electronics that control a hard drive. There are three types currently in use: enhanced small device interface (ESDI), integrated drive electronics (IDE), and small computer system interface (SCSI). *ESDI* and *SCSI* are pronounced *ezdee* and *skuzzy*; IDE is pronounced like the acronym, *I-D-E*. Of the three, ESDI is the oldest standard, but losing ground to IDE, which is less expensive, and to SCSI, which packs both extra speed and intelligence.

Each type of drive must be attached to a disk controller card, although in the case of an IDE drive, most of the electronics that control reading and writing data are contained on the drive itself. The IDE controller card is often a part of the floppy disk controller and contains only the circuitry needed for the drive to communicate with the computer's bus. A SCSI controller is designed for the fastest data transfers, and it contains a coprocessor that relieves the PC's microprocessor of much of the drudgery of overseeing file transfers. In addition, SCSI controllers can also manage tape drives, CD-ROM drives, and even printers; each of the SCSI devices is plugged into another SCSI device, a process called *daisy-chaining*.

Which type of hard drive should you get? Your best bet is the same type of drive you already have in your PC—probably an IDE drive if you bought it in the last few years. The reason is that disk controllers can handle at least two hard drives. By getting the same type of drive that you already have, you avoid using up an additional expansion slot and avoid one more possibility for resource conflicts. If you want maximum performance or if you're planning to expand your system with a CD-ROM drive and a high-capacity (more than 250MB) tape drive, consider a SCSI upgrade. Some IDE controllers will handle CD-ROM drives and tape drives, but they're still relatively rare.

CD-ROM Drive   The CD stands for *compact disk*, just as in the musical CDs that have supplanted vinyl records. The ROM stands for *read-only memory*, which means that you can read data that's been stored on a CD-ROM at the factory, but you can't record any of your own data on it. (There are some writable CDs, but they are far too expensive for most users.) Unlike hard drives, CD-ROMs are not fixed disks. But like a floppy drive, you can remove one CD and replace it with another. Holding up to 600MB of data, CDs are much more capacious than floppies. Their capacity makes them perfect for distributing whole shelves of libraries and for the byte-consuming sound, graphic, and video files that are the meat of multimedia programs. They are also gradually becoming a favored method of distributing software that otherwise could take up dozens of floppies.

Bernoulli Drive   The Bernoulli drive combines the multidisk capabilities of floppy drives with the speed and capacity of hard drives. The disk itself is flexible, and you can remove it and insert another Bernoulli disk. But the disks spin at a much higher rate than floppies do, and in doing so, they produce a hydraulic lift that lets the disk float extremely close to the read/write head without crashing into it (this is called the *Bernoulli effect*). With much of the speed and storage capacity of a hard drive, Bernoulli drives are useful for backups, for storing large amounts of data off-line, and for transferring exceptionally large files among different PCs.

Magneto-Optical and Floptical Drives   These are similar to a writable CD drive, except that the disks used with them are, typically, about half the size and have less capacity. A combination of magnetism and a laser beam allows data to be written to the disk. The drives are useful for backups, for off-line storage, and for transferring files too large to fit on a floppy.

Tape Backup Drive   This should be standard equipment on any PC. There are several types available, including quarter-inch tape (QIC) and DAT (digital audio tape). The kind you have doesn't matter just as long as you have a tape backup. Hard drives these days are too large to back up to floppies, and if you don't back up your data, you are flirting with disaster. Many quarter-inch drives can be used with a floppy controller and hold up to 250MB of data; they are an inexpensive investment.

Despite all the differences among drives, installing any of them in your PC is relatively similar. We'll use a hard drive to illustrate the mounting process, but you can apply the procedures to any type of drive. If you're installing a new controller, you'll need an open expansion slot. If you haven't already read Part 3, review how to install the expansion board now. Here we'll concentrate on the drive itself. Unless you're connecting an external SCSI drive, you need an unused drive bay big enough for the device you're installing, and you'll have to hook up the drive to electrical power and to the controller. Then, if the drive is a hard drive, you'll have to let your system's CMOS know about it, and you may have to use some software that comes with the operating system to initialize the drive.

Before you mount a hard drive, inspect it for any information that will be needed later for the CMOS setup, which we'll cover in the next chapter. The number of cylinders, read/write heads, and other pertinent information is often printed on a label on the outside of the drive itself. Otherwise, the information should be contained in the documentation that came with the drive. If you already have an IDE drive, the second one needs to be configured as a *slave drive* and the original drive needs to be configured as the *master drive*. The configurations are made by changing DIP switches or jumpers on the drives, and the information about which way to set the switches or jumpers is contained on the drives' labels or in their documentation.

Mounting a Drive

1 Select a drive bay that is big enough for the drive you want to install. The drive bay is simply a couple of vertical pieces of sheet metal with a number of slits in them. The idea of the multiple slits is that at least a couple of them will line up with the mounting holes on the sides of the drive. The bays also may have some support tabs for the drive to rest on. The tabs make the process easier, but they aren't essential. In fact, if you don't depend on the tabs you can mount two half-height drives in a single full-height bay.

2 On a desktop PC, remove any expansion cards or cables that block inside access to the drive bays or to the screw slots.

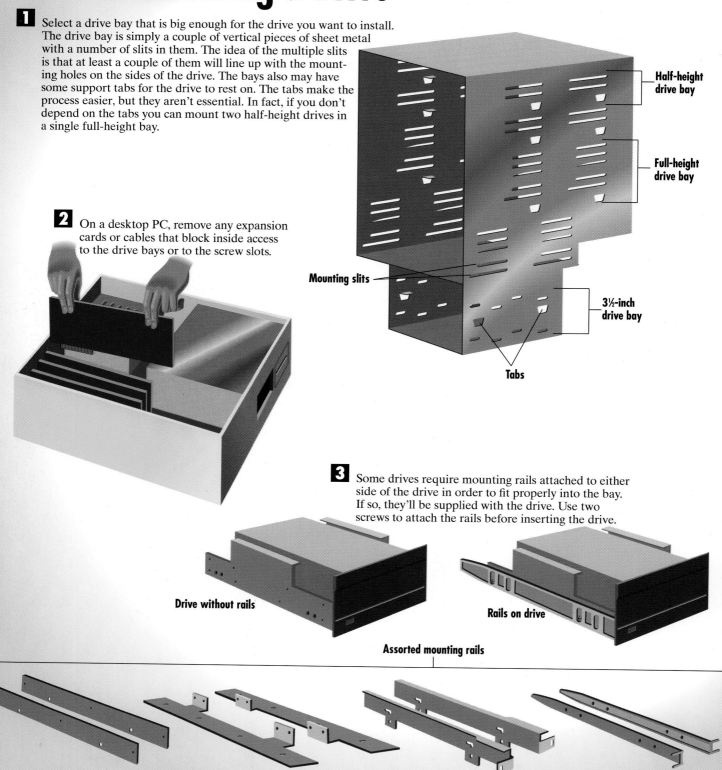

Half-height drive bay

Full-height drive bay

Mounting slits

3½-inch drive bay

Tabs

3 Some drives require mounting rails attached to either side of the drive in order to fit properly into the bay. If so, they'll be supplied with the drive. Use two screws to attach the rails before inserting the drive.

Drive without rails

Rails on drive

Assorted mounting rails

4 From the front of the PC, slide in the drive until the front of the drive is flush with the front of the computer.

5 If the slits on the side of the bay don't line up neatly with the screw holes in the sides of the drive (on in the mounting rails), wiggle the drive a bit to line up the holes while keeping the drive level. Screw in two screws on one side of the drive, and if possible, use two screws on the opposite side. On some desktop PCs, you may be able to use mounting screws on only one side of the drive. As long as the drive is resting on the tabs or the bottom of the bay, screws on only one side are plenty. On tower PCs, where you can usually access the drive bay from both sides, you may be able to ignore the support tabs in order to line up the slits and screw holes. Before putting the final twists to the mounting screws, check the front of the drive to make sure it's still flush with the front of the computer.

Connecting the Wiring

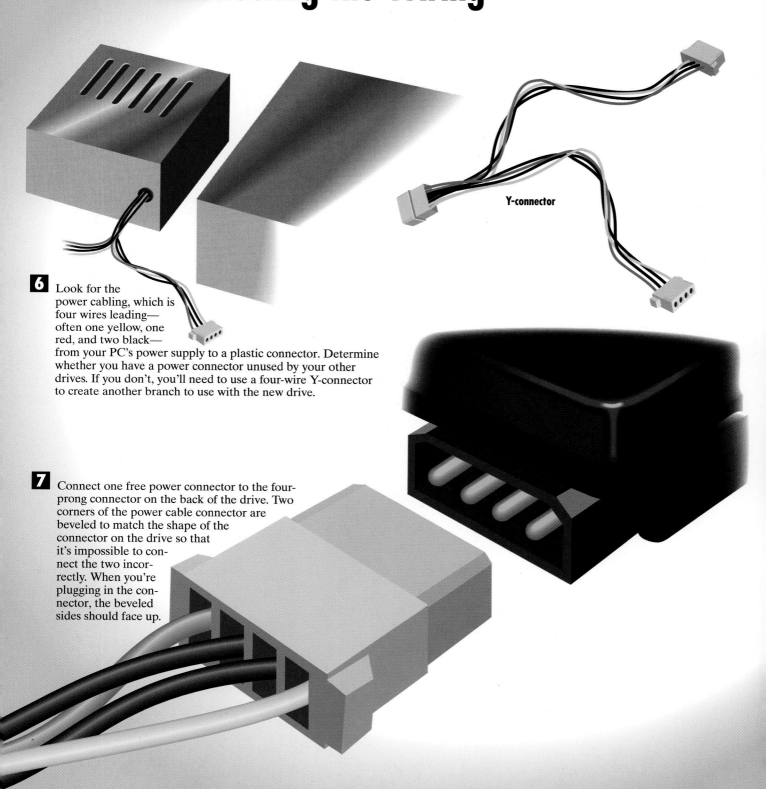

Y-connector

6 Look for the power cabling, which is four wires leading— often one yellow, one red, and two black— from your PC's power supply to a plastic connector. Determine whether you have a power connector unused by your other drives. If you don't, you'll need to use a four-wire Y-connector to create another branch to use with the new drive.

7 Connect one free power connector to the four-prong connector on the back of the drive. Two corners of the power cable connector are beveled to match the shape of the connector on the drive so that it's impossible to connect the two incorrectly. When you're plugging in the connector, the beveled sides should face up.

8 Look for the ribbon cable running from the drive controller. The width of the ribbon and the exact type of connector will depend on the type of drive you're installing. Except on floppy drives, most connectors also have tabs or other devices to prevent you from connecting them the wrong way. If they don't have tabs, look for a colored stripe along one edge of the ribbon cable. The connector should be attached so that the stripe is aligned with the number 1 pin of the drive's connector. A *1* should be stamped on the drive's connector or on the circuit board next to the connector to identify the end with the 1 pin. On hard drives, pin 1 is often on the side closer to the power connector.

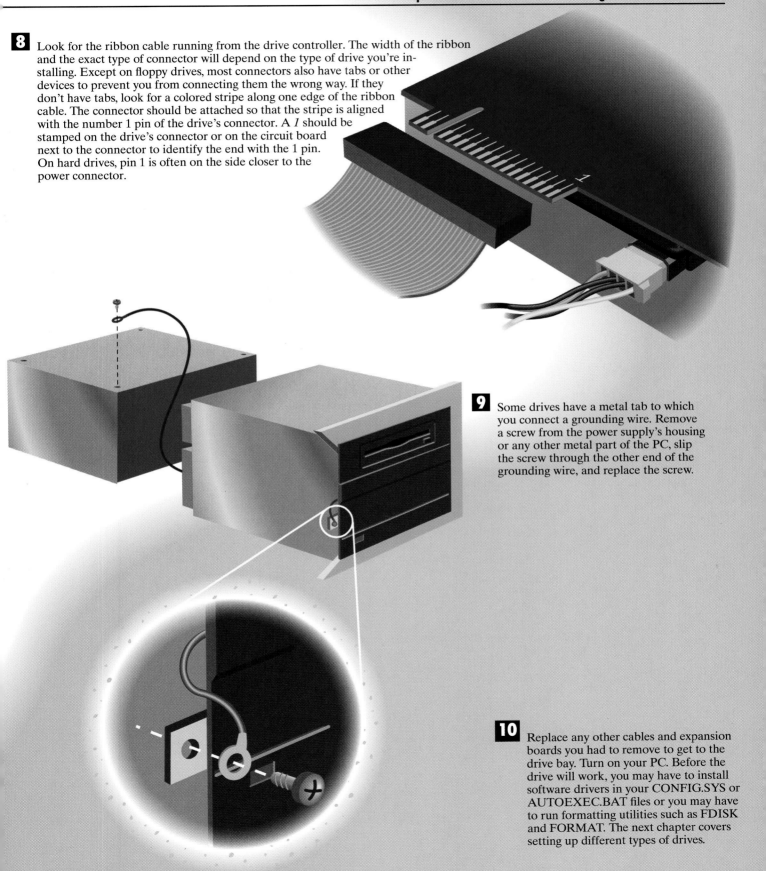

9 Some drives have a metal tab to which you connect a grounding wire. Remove a screw from the power supply's housing or any other metal part of the PC, slip the screw through the other end of the grounding wire, and replace the screw.

10 Replace any other cables and expansion boards you had to remove to get to the drive bay. Turn on your PC. Before the drive will work, you may have to install software drivers in your CONFIG.SYS or AUTOEXEC.BAT files or you may have to run formatting utilities such as FDISK and FORMAT. The next chapter covers setting up different types of drives.

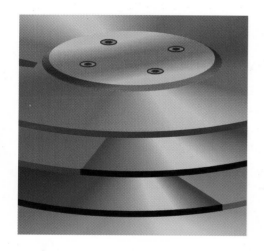

CHAPTER

12

Setting Up a Hard Drive

NOW THAT YOU have installed a drive, you have to let your computer and your operating system know that the drive is out there, and you have to supply enough details about the drive so that your PC knows how to use it.

When the PC was invented, no one could have predicted the many different types of components that would be added to it. But a PC has to have some way to know, for example, the size of a hard drive and how to communicate with a tape drive. There are two ways to supply the missing link between your computer and the new drive you've added: the CMOS setup and device drivers. We've looked at the CMOS earlier in the book, and we'll take a look at it again in the next few pages with a particular emphasis on hard drives. But right now let's look at device drivers.

Device drivers are software code that add to the operating system the capabilities of working with a new hardware device. Occasionally, they may be used with a hard drive, but more often, you'll find device drivers used to supply the missing link between your PC and CD-ROM drives, tape drives, magneto-optical drives, and Bernoulli drives. Device drivers are usually installed in the CONFIG.SYS file that your PC reads when it's booted. Any line in your CONFIG.SYS file that begins DEVICE= loads a device driver. Occasionally a device driver might be loaded in your AUTOEXEC.BAT file. In that case, the driver doesn't use DEVICE= but is loaded with a command name like any other program.

If your new drive requires a device driver, its manual will say so, and the driver will be supplied on a floppy disk. You will need to copy the device driver file to your hard disk and enter the DEVICE= line in CONFIG.SYS that includes the path to the directory where you've saved the driver. You may also need to include some *switches* or *parameters* at the end of the line; these are qualifications to the device driver that make it use specific options. For example, the driver that loads my sound card includes two parameters:

```
DEVICE=C:\PROAUDIO\MVSOUND.SYS D:5 Q:7
```

That line tells the operating system that the driver MVSOUND.SYS, which is found in the directory C:\PROAUDIO, uses DMA channel 5 and interrupt 7. (See Chapter 10 for more information on DMAs and interrupts.) If you need to add any parameters to your drivers, your new drive's manual should explain how to use them, or, better yet, the floppy disk may come with an installation program that tests your system or asks you some questions to determine what parameters to use. It may even add the line to CONFIG.SYS for you. But you should make a backup of CONFIG.SYS and AUTOEXEC.BAT before you install any new drivers and double-check after any installation to find out what's been done to those two crucial files. Installation programs are only semi-smart and often put a new line in the wrong place or delete or add lines they shouldn't.

In you're installing a floppy drive or an ESDI or IDE hard drive, device drivers are usually not needed. But you still need to give your PC some information about ESDI and IDE drives before the PC will be able to handle them. This is done with the CMOS setup. If you are installing a SCSI drive, the SCSI controller takes care of all the messy details of communications between the drive and the PC. But you have to do two things with a SCSI drive that you don't have to with IDE and ESDI drives: Set the SCSI ID number and terminate the last SCSI device on your system. The ID number is needed because a single SCSI controller can handle up to seven devices, but it needs a way to know which is which. The termination identifies the last SCSI device in the daisy chain. And no matter what type of hard drive you have, you'll have to partition it and format it. We'll cover all these steps in this chapter.

Setting Up ESDI and IDE Drives

After installing an ESDI or IDE drive, plug your PC's power cord back in and turn on your computer. When the screen tells you to press a key combination to display the setup screen, press the correct keys for your system. (For more on the CMOS setup, see Chapter 4.)

ROM BIOS (1992)
Press <DEL> to Enter Set-up

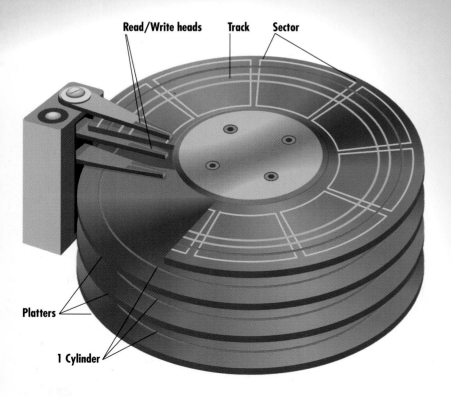

Read/Write heads   Track   Sector

Platters

1 Cylinder

Your computer's CMOS setup needs to know some details about the hard drive. Each hard drive consists of several metal platters, and there is a read/write head for each side of each platter. Each platter is divided radially into sectors and concentrically into tracks. The same tracks on each side of every platter, all together, make up one cylinder. The cylinders, sectors, and tracks are like a road map to the drive so that files can be stored in an organized manner and be found later. Your CMOS setup may want to know the drive's landing zone and capacity, or size. The *landing zone* is made up of specific cylinders where no data is stored. When the read/write heads are at rest, they're positioned over the tracks that make up the landing zone cylinder so that if something should cause the heads to scratch the spinning platters, the heads won't destroy any data.

On new drives, some of the information may be included on a label on the drive. Don't worry if not all of the information is there. If the label or the drive's installation manual includes a drive type, that's all you need to know. Drive types are numbers stored in the PC's BIOS chips. Each number corresponds to a different combination of cylinders, sectors, read/write heads, and so on.

When you display the CMOS setup screen, one of the first items of information you'll see is the hard disk type for the drives. If you know the drive type, you can enter that number, and the rest of the information about the drive will be entered automatically. If you know only a few of the details about the drive, enter them. Often with just a few details, the CMOS setup is able to make a unique match with one of the drive types stored in the BIOS and will finish the job for you. Save the settings and exit the CMOS setup.

Setting Up a SCSI Drive

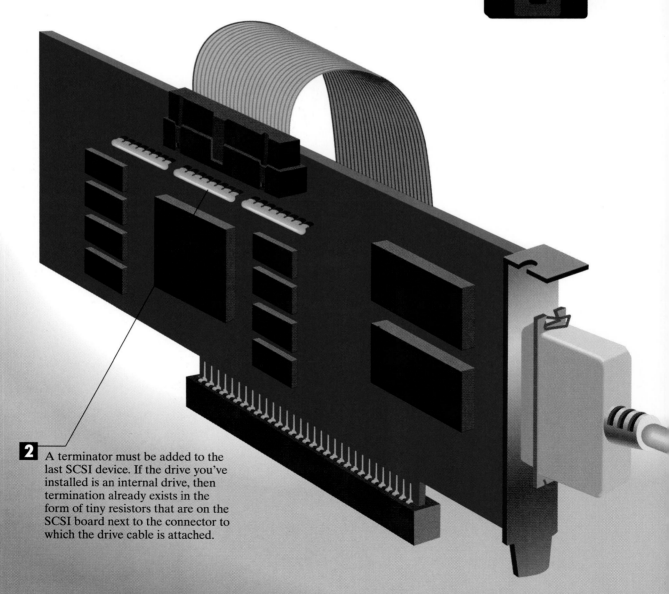

1 Each SCSI device must have a unique ID number between 0 and 7—but the SCSI controller itself uses one of those ID numbers, usually 7. Look for a control like one of the two shown here. Both are used to set the SCSI drive's ID number. For the control on the left, use a small screwdriver to turn the arrow to point to an unused number. For the control on the right, press the buttons above and below the number to increase or decrease the number.

2 A terminator must be added to the last SCSI device. If the drive you've installed is an internal drive, then termination already exists in the form of tiny resistors that are on the SCSI board next to the connector to which the drive cable is attached.

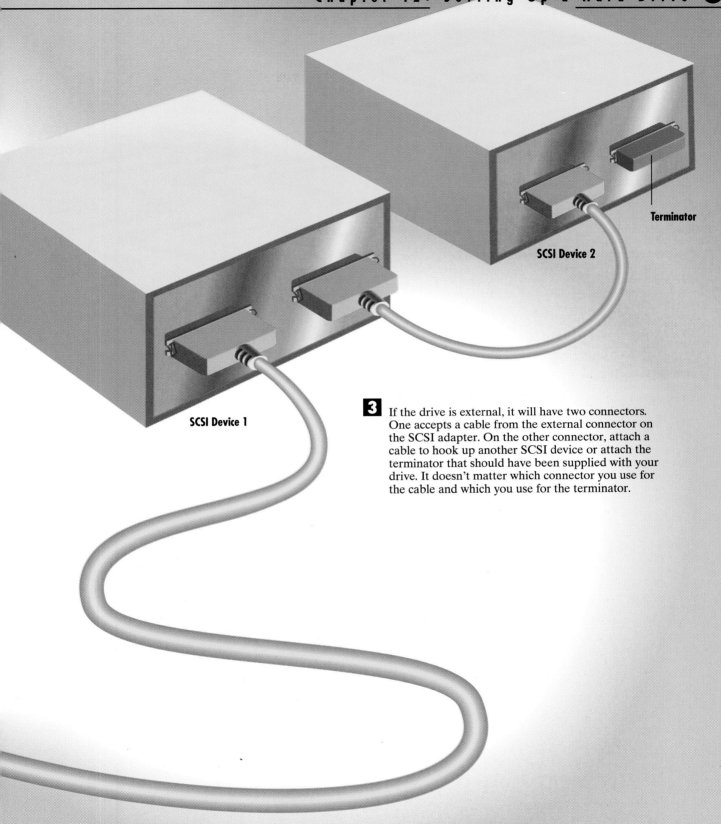

Terminator

SCSI Device 2

SCSI Device 1

3 If the drive is external, it will have two connectors. One accepts a cable from the external connector on the SCSI adapter. On the other connector, attach a cable to hook up another SCSI device or attach the terminator that should have been supplied with your drive. It doesn't matter which connector you use for the cable and which you use for the terminator.

Partitioning and Formatting a Hard Drive

```
              MS-DOS Version 6
            Fixed Disk Setup Program
    (C) Copyright Microsoft Corp. 1983-1993
                 FDISK Options
Current fixed disk drive: 1
Choose one of the following:
1. Create DOS partition or Logical DOS Drive
2. Set active partition


3. Delete partition or Logical DOS Drive

4. Display partition information

5. Change current fixed disk drive
```

```
              Change Current Fixed Disk Drive
Disk    Drv    Mbytes    Free    Usage

 1             203        0      100%

        C:     203



 2             249       249      0%
```

1 After installing any new hard drive, from the C drive (if that's not the one you're installing) or from a DOS floppy disk (if you are installing a C drive), run the program *FDISK*, which stands for *fixed disk*. FDISK configures a hard disk for use with the MS-DOS operating system.

2 If the new drive is in addition to a hard drive that is already in your PC, select the number of the new drive from a menu presented by FDISK. The new drive will always be the highest number.

3 From the next menu that appears, select the option for creating a DOS partition or logical DOS drive. And from the next menu, choose Create Primary DOS Partition. You can create a partition as large as the entire disk or you can choose to create several partitions and create logical drives. Although a logical drive is only part of a real physical drive, the operating system sees it and treats it as if it were a separate physical drive. For example, if you partition your only hard drive into three logical drives, the operating system will see that as drives C, D, and E.

```
                 FDISK Options
Current fixed disk drive: 2
Choose one of the following:
1. Create DOS partition or Logical DOS Drive

2. Set active partition



3. Delete partition or Logical

4. Display partition informat
```

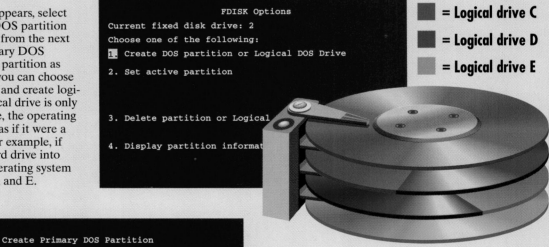

■ = Logical drive C
■ = Logical drive D
■ = Logical drive E

Physical Drive

```
              Create Primary DOS Partition
Current fixed disk drive: 2



Total disk space is 249 Mbytes (1 Mbyte = 1048576 bytes)
Maximum space available for partition is 249 Mbytes (100%)

Enter partition size in Mbytes or percent of disk space (%) to
Create a Primary DOS Partition.....................: [149]

No partitions defined
```

4 If you choose to divide your drive into more than one partition, FDISK will tell you the total amount of space on the new drive and ask how much you want to use for a primary DOS partition. Fill in an answer in either megabytes or as a percentage of the free disk space.

```
             Create Primary DOS Partition
Current fixed disk drive: 2

Partition  Status  Type  Volume Label  Mbytes  System   Usage
D: 1                PRI DOS              149    UNKNOWN   60%




Primary DOS Partition created, drive letters changed or added
```

5 In an instant, FDISK will create the partition, give it the next available drive letter, and display a table with information about the first partition. Notice that under System, the entry is unknown because at this stage, you haven't formatted the drive with DOS or any other operating system.

```
          Create DOS Partition or Logical DOS Drive
Current fixed disk drive: 2

Choose one of the following:

1. Create Primary DOS Partition


2. Create Extended DOS Partition


3. Create Logical DOS Drive(s) in the Extended DOS Partition


Enter choice: [   ]
```

6 If you chose to partition your new drive as one large drive, skip to step 9. But if you chose to divide the drive into more than one logical drive, after creating the primary DOS partition, you have to create an extended DOS partition to hold the remaining logical drives. Follow the steps above beginning with step 3. But this time instead of choosing to create a primary DOS partition, choose the menu item for creating an extended DOS partition.

7 Again, enter the size of the second petition in megabytes or as a percentage of the remaining, uncommitted disk space.

8 After FDISK creates the extended partition, you'll be told that there are no logical drives to define, and you'll be given the opportunity to make all or part of the extended partition into a logical drive. If you choose less than the total space of the extended drive, the process will repeat itself with you creating more logical drives until all the extended partition space is used.

```
             Create Extended DOS Partition
Current fixed disk drive: 2

Partition  Status  Type  Volume Label  Mbytes  System   Usage
 D: 1                PRI DOS             149    UNKNOWN   60%



Total disk space is 249 Mbytes (1 Mbyte = 1048576 bytes)
Maximum space available for partition is 100 Mbytes (40%)

Enter partition size in Mbytes or percent of disk space (%) to
Create an Extended DOS Partition...................: [100]



Press Esc to return to FDISK Options
```

```
    Create Logical DOS Drive(s) in the Extended DOS Partition
Drv  Volume Label  Mbytes  System   Usage

E:                    50    UNKNOWN   50%




Total Extended DOS Partition size is 100 Mbytes (1 Mbyte = 1048576 bytes)
Maximum space available for logical drive is 50 Mbytes (50%)

Enter logical drive size in Mbytes or percent of disk space(%)...[50]
```

9 After partitioning your hard drive, run the DOS FORMAT utility for the logical drive that you created as a primary DOS partition and for each of the logical drives you carved out of the extended DOS partition. Formatting divides the platters of the drive into their tracks and sectors. If you are installing a new C drive, include the /S parameter after the FORMAT command. This transfers the system files to the hard drive so that your computer will be able to load the operating system from the C drive when you turn on your PC.

```
C:\>format d:

WARNING: ALL DATA ON NON-REMOVABLE DISK
DRIVE D: WILL BE LOST!
Proceed with Format (Y/N)?y

Formatting 149.14 M
 12 percent completed
```

HOT TIP Although you can partition a hard drive into one large drive, it's easier to manage your files if you partition it into two or more logical drives. By dividing a single physical drive into two logical drives, you can, for example, keep all your programs on logical drive C and all your data files on logical drive D. Because you can always restore your programs from their original distribution disks, this means that you only have to back up drive D to protect your data. Also, if your physical drive is larger than 250MB, breaking it into logical drives, each smaller than 250MB, allows you to back up the drives using inexpensive tape backups that are often limited to 250MB at a time.

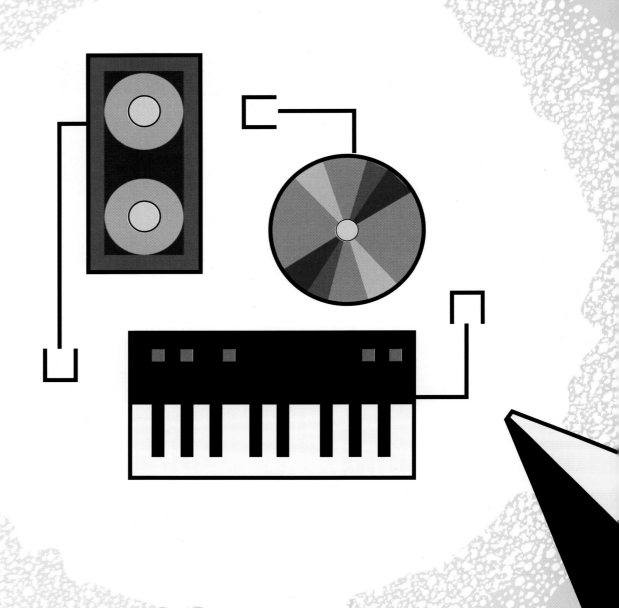

MULTIMEDIA

CONTENTS

N RECENT YEARS multimedia has extended the capabilities of personal computers more than has any other technology. And no technology has had as little practical application as multimedia. The business uses for multimedia have been few; presentations and training are the most notable. Sound and video more often find their ways into games and educational products than they do into the bread-and-butter applications that justify the cost of computers.

You know what? I don't care that multimedia technology isn't practical yet—and neither do the more than 10 million people who have bought CD-ROMs and sound cards in the last few years. Multimedia is too enjoyable not to want it. Sound makes your PC come alive. Mine tells me the time, speaks up to remind me of appointments, and shouts when I'm running low on drive space. Oh, if you insist, there are more practical applications for sound, too. You can use it to issue spoken commands to your applications. Or you can let it read back numbers you're typing into a spreadsheet. Or you can clarify instructions by adding a spoken annotation to a file that you send to a coworker.

Video is a bit rougher to justify. Full-motion video, which also includes sound, takes up enormous amounts of disk space and processing time. To alleviate the problem, most video appears in a tiny window that uses only a fraction of your screen, and it tends to be jerky on some systems. Those problems are on the way out, though. Although not yet in wide use, a video format called MPEG (for Motion Picture Expert Group) compresses full-screen video files to a more practical size for everyday hard drives. And faster processors and faster video boards are making jerkiness, like that of silent movies, a thing of the past.

Video has yet to find a killer business application, but it is an enormous boon to educational and personal-interest software. A video or animation can explain in seconds what thousands of words would fail to convey. You can see the flight of birds, the movements of armies, the flow of blood, the inner workings of PCs—any process in which the passage of time aids the explanation. If you can also see the Beatles' *A Hard Day's Night* or *It's a Wonderful Life* on your PC, that's all the better.

If you are going to upgrade your PC to accommodate multimedia, you should purchase components that are certified to meet MPC Level 2 specifications, a set of standards issued by the Multimedia PC Marketing Council. The standards, basically, specify that a sound card must be compatible with the Sound Blaster brand sound card, and that a CD-ROM drive be able to transfer data at 300K a second while using no more than 60 percent of the CPU's processing time. Nearly all sound cards come with Sound

Blaster compatibility, and most CD drives designated 2× speed drives meet the speed qualification. You can get by with a VGA video adapter and monitor. But consider purchasing a super VGA setup. Super VGA is capable of displaying more than 600 pixels by 400 pixels and at least 256 colors. Some multimedia programs will not work properly with only the standard 16 colors of VGA.

You can buy the components individually or you can find several multimedia upgrade kits that include a sound card, speakers, a SCSI adapter, and a CD-ROM drive. Provided that the individual components of the kits are MPC 2–compliant, they can be a bargain. The components will work together, which is not always true if you mix-and-match on your own. The speakers are usually nothing to rave about, but they're as good as you'll find on a lot of boom boxes. Plus, often a lot of multimedia disks are bundled with it. If the price is right, go for a kit.

No matter how you get the components, setting up your system for multimedia capability involves four steps—installing the CD-ROM drive, installing the sound card, attaching the speakers, and installing software. We'll cover all these steps in the next three chapters.

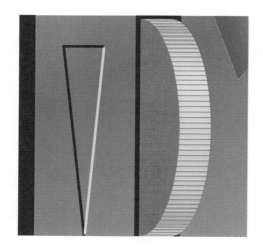

CHAPTER 13

Installing a Sound Card

THERE IS SOMETHING uncanny about a machine that can talk to you. And I don't mean a TV or CD player. They only make the sounds that are fed into them. You know what to expect. But a computer with a sound card can say things, or just make weird noises, at unexpected times. With a PC, sound is not just something you listen to passively; it's a form of communication, a way you and your PC interact. It has its musical side, too. It can make a C-sharp sound of a piano or a bassoon. But it's the ability of a PC to provide vocal feedback on what you're doing that makes it seem not so much that you're using a PC but that you're working in partnership with one.

If you're transforming your PC into a multimedia machine, it's the sound card that will give it life. Sure, videos on screen are fine, but they're still canned material. And a CD-ROM drive is necessary because both sound and videos chew up disk space like mad. But it's the sound card that's going to really make a difference in how you use and enjoy your PC.

If sound is where the fun is, it's also where the frustration can be. In theory, you should be able to set up a sound card with IRQ, DMA, and memory settings that don't conflict with any of your other expansion cards, and that should be it. But I review about 15–25 CDs a month for *PC/Computing* magazine, and I've found huge differences in how software companies handle sound. I've found no settings that work for all circumstances. One group of settings works fine for one CD, but on another CD, they make voices sound as if someone's playing with the speaker's adam's apple—although the music sounds great. Unless your job involves looking at as many multimedia disks as my job does, don't let my experiences discourage you. Particularly if you work primarily within Windows, you won't run into problems as often as I do.

Part of the reason for the need for different settings is that there are four ways in which a sound card can produce sound. Within Windows, one of the most common ways is by using files with the extension .WAV. These are digital recordings of sounds that the software sends directly to a chip called a *digital-to-analog converter (DAC)*. The DAC compares each digital number in the file to a table of analog voltage values and sends that value to your speakers. A *MIDI (musical instrument digital interface)* file includes instructions used to identify a note to be played, such as

D-sharp, and an instrument to play that note, for example, a trumpet. It uses stored sample recordings of different instruments to produce the sound. FM synthesis uses a mathematical algorithm to approximate the sounds of a musical instrument. On top of all this, some CD-ROMs mix in music that's recorded in the same manner as ordinary music compact disks. These CDs may bypass your PC entirely and feed music tracks directly to the sound card or headphones.

If you're considering buying a sound card for your PC, there are a few things you should look for. It should be compatible with the Sound Blaster card from Creative Labs, the de facto standard for sound cards. Any multimedia program will work with a Sound Blaster or compatible card. Try to get a card with a *digital signal processor* (DSP)—a processor that can be reprogrammed on the fly. It relieves some of the processing burden from your CPU, and it allows your sound card to be upgraded with software without you even taking the card out of your PC. A SCSI port is not necessarily a desirable extra. Some of the SCSI connections on sound cards don't support the faster transfer rates of hard drives, although they will work fine with the slower CD-ROM drives. Of course, if you're running out of expansion slots and don't intend to get a SCSI hard drive, a sound card's SCSI port is OK. Finally, the sound card should be a 16-bit card rather than the older 8-bit type. A 16-bit card creates more faithful sound reproduction.

Whatever card you buy, the process of installing it and getting it to work is pretty much the same. That's what we'll cover in the next pages. There's a little cart-and-horse problem here because some of these instructions depend on having speakers hooked up, which isn't covered until the next chapter. You may want to read all the chapters in this section before you start the installation.

Adding a Sound Card

1 Before you get started, check your sound card's manual for information on the DMA, IRQ, and upper-memory block settings that it can use, and make sure the manual and the factory settings agree. Sound cards typically can use DMA channels 1, 3, and 10, although I've also got them to work with DMA 5 and 7 at times. Various cards may use any of the 15 interrupt settings and any of several memory address ranges. If you need a refresher on these terms or if you skipped Chapter 10 entirely, go back to it for an explanation of how these PC resources can lead to conflicts among expansion cards. If you filled out the resource records in Chapter 10, check whether any of the cards you already have are using settings favored by your new sound card—and whether there are alternatives you can use on either of the conflicting cards. Make any necessary jumper or DIP-switch changes.

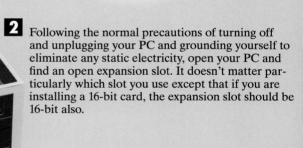

2 Following the normal precautions of turning off and unplugging your PC and grounding yourself to eliminate any static electricity, open your PC and find an open expansion slot. It doesn't matter particularly which slot you use except that if you are installing a 16-bit card, the expansion slot should be 16-bit also.

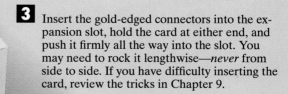

3 Insert the gold-edged connectors into the expansion slot, hold the card at either end, and push it firmly all the way into the slot. You may need to rock it lengthwise—*never* from side to side. If you have difficulty inserting the card, review the tricks in Chapter 9.

4 Screw down the tab that meets the rail at the back of the PC. Reattach any cables you had to remove to gain access to the expansion slot, but don't put the cover back on your PC yet. After doing the software installation, if you run into problems, you may need to remove it to change settings.

5 If the sound card has an external volume control on the end of the card, turn it all the way up. Most software provides a way to control volume that will let you turn it down, but the software can't make the sound any louder than its loudest physical setting.

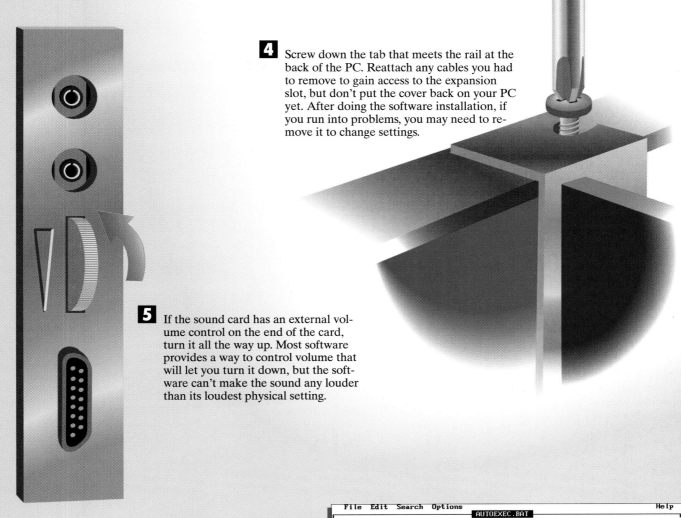

```
 File  Edit  Search  Options                                           Help
                            ┌─────── AUTOEXEC.BAT ───────┐
C:\CORELDRV\CORELCDX /M:8 /E:3 /D:MSCD001                                    ↑
REM  THE CHECK LINE BELOW PROVIDES ADDITIONAL SAFETY FOR STACKER DRIVES.
REM  PLEASE DO NOT REMOVE IT.
C:\STACKER\CHECK /WP
C:\DOS\SMARTDRV.EXE /L /X
SET GSFONTS=C:\GSFONTS
SET BLASTER=A220 I7 D1 T2
SET SOUND=C:\SBPRO
set temp=c:\windows\temp
prompt $p$g
echo PATH=C:\WINDOWS;C:\WPWIN60;C:\WPC20;c:\winword;C:\DATA\NOTES;C:\BAT;C:\DO
call c:\setpath.bat
NUMOFF
pause
rem goto end
C:
CD C:\TOOLS
SYSCTRL
CD \
c:\qemm\loadhi /r:2 c:\pcache\pcache
win                                                                          ↓
←┤                                                                         →
MS-DOS Editor   <F1=Help>  Press ALT to activate menus             00008:019
```

6 Turn on your PC and see if it works normally. If it doesn't, double-check the resource settings of all your cards for conflicts and try again. If the PC boots normally, make copies of your AUTOEXEC.BAT and CONFIG.SYS files, and then run the installation software that came with the sound card. This normally will add a line to your CONFIG.SYS or AUTOEXEC.BAT files that loads the software driver to let the card and your operating system communicate. The line may also include settings for DMA, IRQ, and UMB address. The screen to the right shows two highlighted lines in my AUTOEXEC.BAT used by my Sound Blaster card. The first tells the system that the sound card will be using a memory range beginning at hexadecimal A220, IRQ 7, and DMA 1. The *T2* refers to the model of the card. These settings should, of course, agree with the settings established on the card with DIP switches or jumpers. The second line tells other programs the name of the directory in which the Sound Blaster software is located.

NOTE The sound card you use will have variations on these commands. Follow the instructions in your manual or the installation program. Then reboot your PC so the start-up files take effect, look for any signs of conflicts, and if you're not using Windows, test the sound capabilities with a DOS multimedia program or one of the test programs that probably came with your sound card.

Making a Sound Card Work with Windows

1 If you are using Windows, the installation program may complete the necessary modifications to the Windows system files to make the driver available under Windows. Even if it does, though, you should know how to update and change the driver's setting manually if you find that the installed DMA, IRQ, and other settings don't work. The process starts by double-clicking the Control Panel icon in the Windows Program Manager.

Control Panel

2 Within Control Panel, double-click the Drivers icon.

Drivers

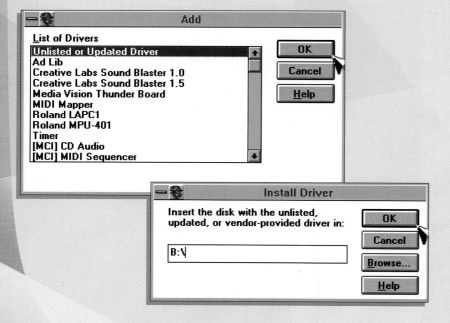

Add

List of Drivers

Unlisted or Updated Driver
Ad Lib
Creative Labs Sound Blaster 1.0
Creative Labs Sound Blaster 1.5
Media Vision Thunder Board
MIDI Mapper
Roland LAPC1
Roland MPU-401
Timer
[MCI] CD Audio
[MCI] MIDI Sequencer

OK
Cancel
Help

Install Driver

Insert the disk with the unlisted, updated, or vendor-provided driver in:

B:\

OK
Cancel
Browse...
Help

3 Click on Add, and when the Add dialog box appears, select the driver you need to install, and click on OK. The Driver dialog box will appear asking you to insert a Windows installation disk or a disk that came with the sound card. But if the Add dialog doesn't list the driver you need, select Unlisted or Updated Drivers and click OK to produce the Install Driver dialog box. It asks you for the name of the drive on which the new driver can be found—usually A or B.

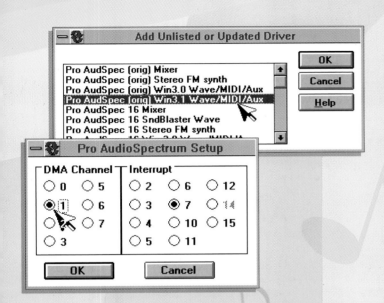

4 Select the driver for your sound card and click OK. You may be asked to set up DMA, IRQ, or memory settings. Start off with the same settings you used in CONFIG.SYS or AUTOEXEC.BAT to set up the card. But you don't have to end up with the same settings. You may find that some combinations of DMA and IRQ at the boot-up level work best with DOS-only programs, and other settings may work better for Windows-controlled sounds.

5 After you finished the installation, Control Panel will prompt you that Windows needs to be restarted. Chose the restart button and when Windows is back up, test the system sounds you can use by selecting Sounds from the Control Panel. If the sounds don't sound right, try different combinations of resource settings—being sure to change only one setting at a time—until you find a combination that works best.

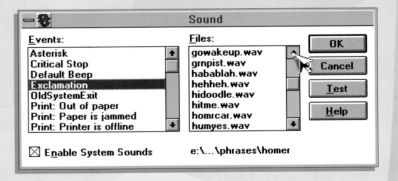

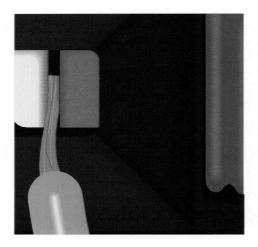

CHAPTER 14

Installing Speakers

YOUR PC CAN only get better when you add multimedia speakers to it. Even if you buy the cheapest, worst pair of speakers you can find, they're still going to be better than the puny speaker that's been the standard in PCs for more than a decade. And even if you're too clumsy to tie your own shoes, you can hook up your speakers faster than you can program a VCR.

Of course, you can't just hook up any speakers to your sound card. Ordinarily, the speakers used with a multimedia PC include a built-in amplifier because the signal that the sound card produces is unamplified. Hooking the card directly to ordinary speakers would be like attaching a tape deck to stereo speakers without routing it through the stereo's amplifier. Of course, that's the other option—connecting the sound card to a stereo amplifier and from there, to ordinary speakers. In this chapter, we'll look at both ways of hooking up speakers.

Although even the cheapest speakers are an improvement over the PC's native speaker, you can get still better sound with more expensive speakers, some of which rival the quality (and price) of normal sound-system speakers, down to a separate subwoofer for resounding bass. And you can get more knobs to twirl in addition to the volume control that comes on most multimedia speakers.

For many people, a volume control may be all that they need. Now, I admit I'm gadget happy, but some of the extra controls really can be handy. Most commonly, they let you control balance and pitch. But the control I've found most helpful is one that lets you mix signals from two sources. If a multimedia program uses music tracks of the type found on noncomputer CDs, those tracks are not routed through your PC. Instead, although the tracks can be heard through headphones attached directly to the CD-ROM drive, the only ways to amplify the sound through the speakers is if the speakers have inputs for separate sound sources, or if you make single inputs do double duty with an adapter. The mixer control lets you adjust the loudness of both power sources, which is often necessary so one channel doesn't overpower the other.

Whatever kind of speakers you buy, the instructions here will easily get you through their installation. If all the cables you need for your particular configuration didn't come with your speakers, you can readily find the cables and adapter shown here at any electronics store.

Installing Speakers

Types of Controls

Not all speakers have all the following controls. Yours should be labeled similarly.

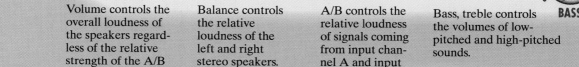

VOLUME LOUD

BALANCE L R

A/B A B

BASS/TREBLE LO HI

TREBLE

BASS

Volume controls the overall loudness of the speakers regardless of the relative strength of the A/B channels.

Balance controls the relative loudness of the left and right stereo speakers.

A/B controls the relative loudness of signals coming from input channel A and input channel B.

Bass, treble controls the volumes of low-pitched and high-pitched sounds.

Types of Connectors

Not all speakers have all these connections. The different types may be found on the same speakers. The following are shown actual size.

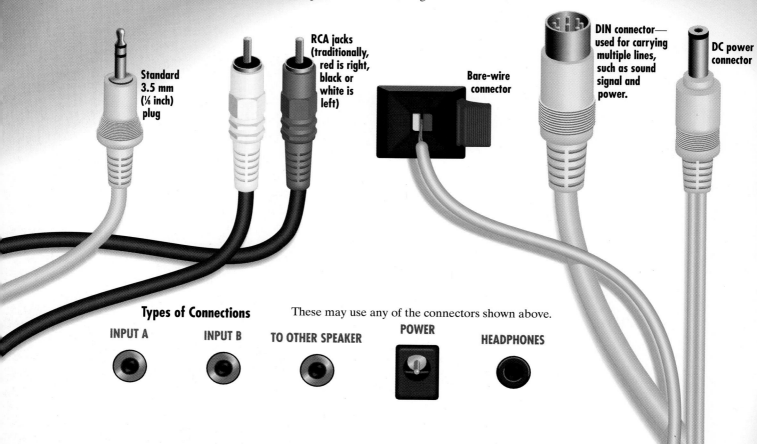

Standard 3.5 mm (⅛ inch) plug

RCA jacks (traditionally, red is right, black or white is left)

Bare-wire connector

DIN connector— used for carrying multiple lines, such as sound signal and power.

DC power connector

Types of Connections

These may use any of the connectors shown above.

INPUT A

INPUT B

TO OTHER SPEAKER

POWER

HEADPHONES

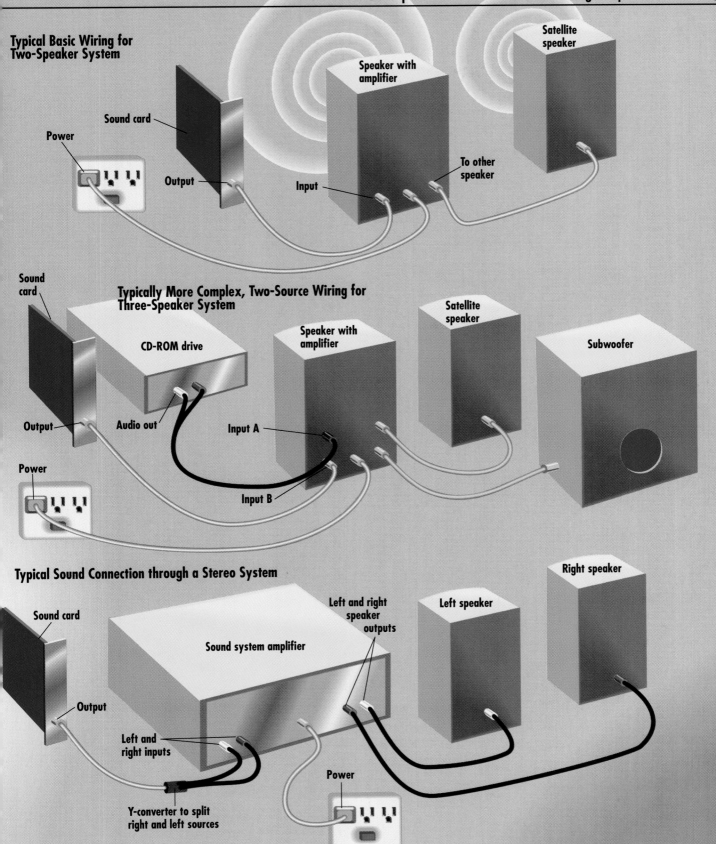

Typical Basic Wiring for Two-Speaker System

Power

Sound card

Output

Speaker with amplifier

Satellite speaker

Input

To other speaker

Typically More Complex, Two-Source Wiring for Three-Speaker System

Sound card

CD-ROM drive

Output

Audio out

Power

Input A

Input B

Speaker with amplifier

Satellite speaker

Subwoofer

Typical Sound Connection through a Stereo System

Sound card

Output

Sound system amplifier

Left and right inputs

Y-converter to split right and left sources

Power

Left and right speaker outputs

Left speaker

Right speaker

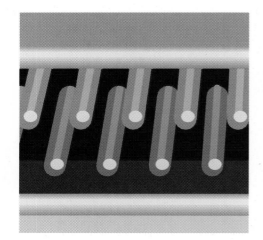

Installing a CD-ROM Drive

F YOU'VE BEEN reading this book from start to finish and already know most of the tricks for installing any kind of drive, including CD-ROM drives, you can then give this chapter a cursory once-over. But if you turned immediately to this section because you just bought a multimedia upgrade kit and you want to install it now, you still came to the right place. This chapter will cover the basics about installing a SCSI adapter and CD drive.

Nearly all CD-ROM drives are SCSI devices. A new breed of IDE controller also manages IDE CD-ROM drives, but these have yet to become common. Even among SCSI drives, there is a lot of variety. Most significantly, they have various rates of transferring data, ranging from 150K per second (1X), to 300Kps (2X), 450Kps (3X), and 600Kps (4X). To be compliant with the latest multimedia standard, you should get a 2X drive. But as far as installing a drive, its speed is irrelevant; you don't do anything differently. The same is true if the drive holds only one disk at a time or if it's a *CD jukebox*, a drive that holds several disks and shuffles each one into position to be read as it's called for. The only significant difference in how a CD drive is installed is whether it's an external or internal drive. External drives take up some desk space and cost a bit more because you're paying for a housing and power supply, but they're easier to set up.

Regardless of the type of CD-ROM drive, you first need to complete three steps: **(1)** Install a SCSI controller, if you don't already have one, and connect the CD-ROM drive to the controller either internally or externally. You have to connect power to the drive, internally, from the PC's power supply and externally, to a surge-protected electrical wall outlet. **(2)** If the drive has a separate audio output, connect that to one of the A/B inputs on the speakers. If you skipped Chapter 12, check it out for tips on installing drivers. The example there is for audio drivers, but the principle is the same. **(3)** Install software drivers in CONFIG.SYS and AUTOEXEC.BAT.

If you do already have a SCSI card installed, skip the next two pages. If you don't, you need to install a SCSI adapter. Most CD-ROM drives can be bought with a SCSI adapter. A few CD drives have non-SCSI proprietary controllers, which can't be used to handle any other hard or CD drives. Get a drive that uses a standard SCSI interface—specifically one that is Adaptec compatible. Adaptec is the de facto standard in SCSI controllers. Some sound cards provide SCSI interfaces, and it's OK to use them for CD drives, but the SCSI interface on a sound card may be too slow for a hard drive.

Take normal precautions by turning off your system, unplugging it, and touching metal to ground yourself before removing the cover of your PC. Select an expansion slot for the card. Most SCSI controllers are ISA, 16-bit cards. If you're going to install an internal drive, try to use an expansion slot that doesn't have a card in the slot above it on a tower model, or to the left of it as you face the back of a desktop PC. The internal cable to the drive must attach to a connector on the top (left) side of the card. It can be a tight squeeze.

Remove the screw holding the metal plate covering the PC's back opening that matches the empty slot you're using and remove and safely store the plate. Then position the board so that its connector edge is lined up with the slot and with your thumbs at either end of the card, press firmly until you feel the card slip into the slot. If the card is inserted properly, the screw tab will be lying flush against the metal railing, to which the tab is screwed.

If the card will not go into the slot or if the screw tab doesn't rest flat against the railing, the most likely problem is a second metal tab at the bottom of the card. Remove the card and using your fingers, bend the tab out slightly. Try reinserting the card, and if it still won't fit, bend the tab in the opposite direction.

Once the card is inserted, wait to screw it down until you've turned on your PC. If there are no conflicts with other cards, your PC should boot as it always has except that a new message will be displayed that identifies the BIOS included on the SCSI card. If there is a problem with the card, you may need to remove it to change jumpers or dip switch settings. Once you're satisfied it's working properly, turn off your PC and screw down the card. If you're installing an internal CD drive, you can replace the cover.

Setting, Mounting, and Cabling CD-ROM Drives

Setting the SCSI ID Number

Select a SCSI ID number from 0 to 6 that doesn't duplicate the number for any other SCSI device on your system. (If this will be the only SCSI device on your system, you can use the factory setting and skip this step.) The SCSI controller itself is usually 7. Check your drive's manual to find out how to select the drive's SCSI setting. Here are the three ways to set the number.

Use a screwdriver to turn the pointer to a number.

Press up and down buttons to raise or lower a number displayed in a window.

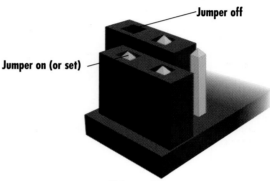

Jumper off

Jumper on (or set)

Join or disconnect some jumpers.

Mounting an Internal Drive

1 Select a half-height drive bay in which to install the CD-ROM drive. Unless the drive is a jukebox model, you won't need a full-height bay. Drive bays are simply a few sheets of metal connected to create some berths in which drives can rest on metal floors or tabs. Some drive bays don't provide access to a drive's front panel, which is fine for a hard drive. But because you have to be able to insert CDs into a CD-ROM drive, make sure that the drive bay is easily accessible from the front of your PC.

Drive accessible from front of PC

Mounting slits

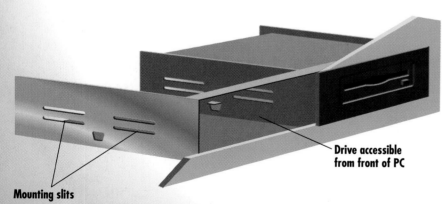

2 Remove any expansion cards, cables, or other drives that block access to the drive bay you want to use. From the front of the PC, slide in the CD drive until the front of it is flush with the front of the computer.

3 Make sure that the slits on the side of the bay panel line up with the screw holes in the sides of the drive. Wiggle the drive around a bit if you need to line up the screw holes. Screw in at least two screws to secure the drive, preferably on opposite sides of the drive. If this is not possible, as is the case in many desktop PCs, try to place two screws in the one side you can get to. Before turning the screws the last couple of turns, check the front of the drive to make sure it's still flush with the front of the computer.

Cabling an Internal CD Drive

1 Connect the four-wire power cabling from your PC's power supply to the drive. The cabling ends in a plastic-encased, four-prong connector. The two corners of the connector that should usually face up are beveled to match the connector on the CD drive; you can't plug it in the wrong way. If you don't have an unused power connector, use a Y-connector to create another branch from a power connector already in use.

Y-connector

2 Connect one end of a ribbon cable supplied with your SCSI card or the drive to a 50-prong connector on the back of the drive. Connect the other end of the ribbon to a similar connector on the SCSI card. Most connectors have tabs or indentations that prevent you from connecting them the wrong way. If yours don't have these tabs, look for a stripe along one edge of the ribbon cable. The stripe indicates the number 1 wire. The side of the ribbon's connector with the stripe leading to it should plug into the number 1 pin on the connectors, on both the drive and SCSI card. There should be a *1* stamped on the connectors or on the circuit boards next to the connectors to identify the ends that have the 1 pin. Generally pin 1 on the drive is located closer to the power-supply connection.

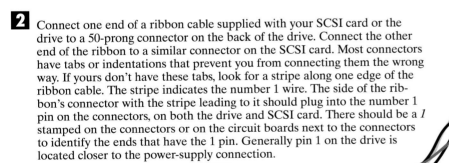

3 Reconnect all cables, drives and expansion boards that you remove.

Installing an External CD-ROM Drive

1 Select a location for the drive that's easily accessible.

2 Attach one end of a SCSI cable to the external port on the back of your SCSI adapter. The cable connector should look like one of these shown here, depending on the type of port on the card.

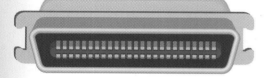

Centronics
The most common SCSI connector is one that looks like an oversize printer connection.

DB25-pin
Identical to a serial cable connector. The connector should be male or female, whichever is the opposite of the connector on the SCSI adapter.

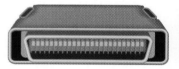

SCSI 2
Relatively rare, but becoming more prevalent.

3 Connect the other end of the cable to either of the external ports on the CD-ROM drive. Fasten the cable on both ends using the screws in the connectors or the wire brackets attached to the adapter and drive ports. SCSI 2 connectors have locks built into them that engage automatically. To release a SCSI 2 connector, squeeze both small sides of it as you pull.

4 If the CD-ROM drive is the last SCSI device daisy-chained to the adapter, plug a terminator into the second connector on the drive. The *terminator* tells the adapter that there are no other devices it needs to control. If the CD-ROM drive is not the last SCSI device, run another cable from the remaining SCSI connector to a port on the other device, and terminate whatever is the last device in the chain.

Terminator

To PC

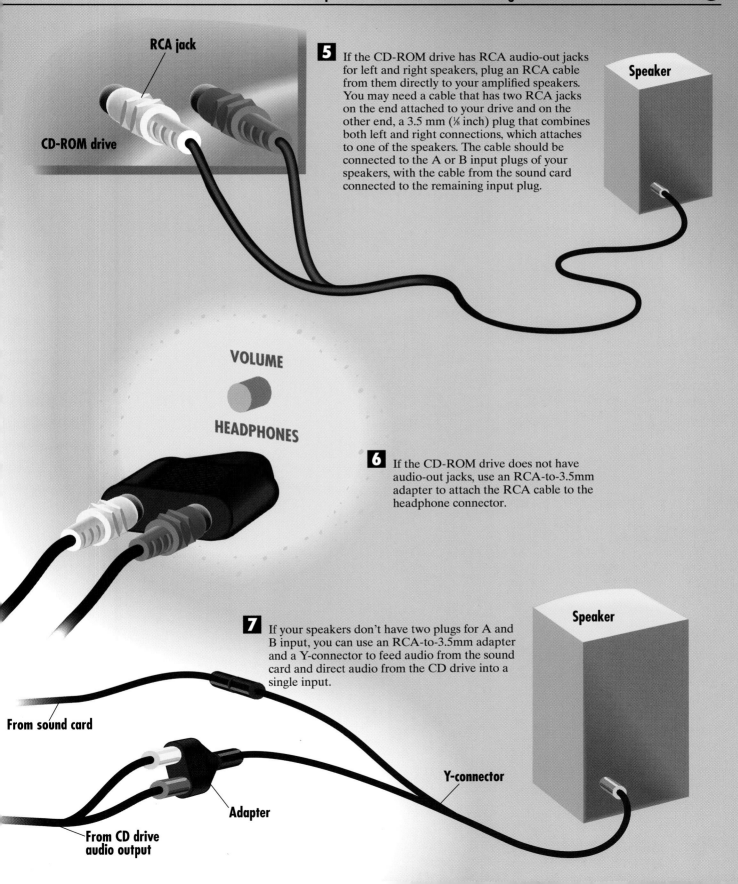

5 If the CD-ROM drive has RCA audio-out jacks for left and right speakers, plug an RCA cable from them directly to your amplified speakers. You may need a cable that has two RCA jacks on the end attached to your drive and on the other end, a 3.5 mm (⅛ inch) plug that combines both left and right connections, which attaches to one of the speakers. The cable should be connected to the A or B input plugs of your speakers, with the cable from the sound card connected to the remaining input plug.

6 If the CD-ROM drive does not have audio-out jacks, use an RCA-to-3.5mm adapter to attach the RCA cable to the headphone connector.

7 If your speakers don't have two plugs for A and B input, you can use an RCA-to-3.5mm adapter and a Y-connector to feed audio from the sound card and direct audio from the CD drive into a single input.

Installing CD-ROM Drivers

Included with your CD-ROM drive should be a floppy disk that contains the drivers needed so that the operating system and the CD drive can communicate with each other. If software isn't provided, buy Corel SCSI Pro, a set of excellent generic drivers and assorted utilities that you can use with most CD drives.

Most of the software that comes with a CD drive also includes an installation program that will copy the drivers to your hard drive and make the necessary changes to your CONFIG.SYS and AUTOEXEC.BAT files to recognize those drivers. Even though all this automation means you won't have to participate actively, it will help in troubleshooting to be at least familiar with how drivers are set up. As always, before installing new software, make copies of your AUTOEXEC.BAT and CONFIG.SYS files, just in case.

The driver that comes with your CD-ROM drive is loaded in CONFIG.SYS. It contains code that tells the operating system the hardware particulars of your CD drive. Most of the parameters don't require you to do anything with them. My CONFIG.SYS, for example, includes the line

```
Device=C:\PIONEER\DRD60ASP.SYS /D:MSCD000 /N:6 /S:2 /C:CDP
```

/S:2 tells the driver the SCSI ID number of my CD drive. It was added automatically by the installation program. The one parameter that you should be familiar with is the one that begins */D:* because the combination of letters and numbers that follow it—in this instance, MSCD000—is called a *driver signature*. It must match a driver signature used in AUTOEXEC.BAT.

In your AUTOEXEC.BAT file, you must include a line that loads the DOS program MSCDEX.EXE, which adds the DOS CD drive extensions to the operating system. For details on the command, you can get much more information than you will ever want to know by typing HELP MSCDEX at the command prompt in DOS 5.0 or later. The one thing you really need to know is that the driver signature in the MSCDEX line in AUTOEXEC.BAT must match the driver signature used in CONFIG.SYS. My AUTOEXEC.BAT file, for example, has the line

```
C:\DOS\MSCDEX.EXE /D:MSCD000
```

Note how the */D:MSCD000* matches the same setting in CONFIG.SYS. Another CD-ROM drive might be configured with */D:MSCD001* in both files.

After the installation, make sure your CD driver is turned on if it's an external drive, and reboot your PC so that the new commands in CONFIG.SYS and AUTOEXEC.BAT can take effect. Put a compact disk in the CD drive; for most drives, this means placing the disk in a *caddy* designed to protect it, and then pushing the caddy into a slot on the front of the drive.

When you get to a DOS prompt, type **DIR x:**, where *x* is the letter of your CD-ROM drive. Ordinarily, the CD drive is automatically given the next available drive letter. If, for example, you have one physical hard drive and it's divided into two logical drives—C and D—the CD drive is assigned E. If you have the LASTDRIVE command in your CONFIG.SYS file, make sure that it specifies a letter after the one your CD drive should receive. If the installation has gone properly, your screen should display the root directory of the CD.

Although CD-ROM drives are by nature slow, you can easily speed up their transfer rates by using a disk cache that will work with CD-ROM drives. The cache reads extra data from a drive each time the disk is read and holds that data in RAM. Often the next read request is for the data already in memory, and the drive doesn't have to be accessed. Both PC-Kwik and Helix make excellent disk caches that work with CD-ROM disks. But MS-DOS 6.2 supplies a disk cache, SMARTDRV.EXE, which caches CDs also. The only trick to SMARTDRV is that it must be loaded after the MSCDEX command in AUTOEXEC.BAT. When SMARTDRV is loaded properly, it automatically senses the presence of a CD drive and caches it without further instructions from you.

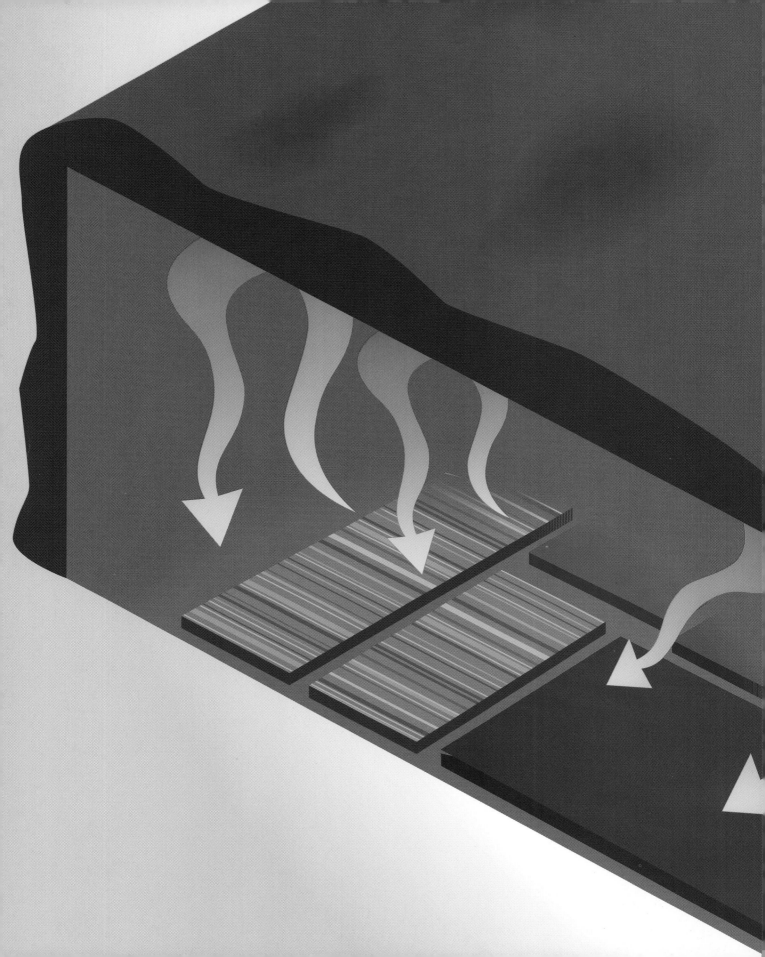

KEEPING YOUR PC RUNNING

CONTENTS

OVERVIEW

I T'S MIDNIGHT. YOU'RE busy working on that report you have to present to the board tomorrow morning. This is big; your whole career's riding on it. And...and... everything you type appears on your PC's screen as gibberish! Or your printer puts every letter on a separate page! Or your system refuses to recognize the drive where you've stored all the supporting spreadsheets!

And who are you going to call in the middle of the night? The repair shops are closed. You don't have the home number of the office PC guru. You're on your own.

Relax. There's a good chance—a very good chance—you'll get your system running again, make it through the night, and wow the board of directors. Just as I hope the previous chapters have shown you, there's nothing mysterious or mystical about installing PC components. This section is devoted to showing you the equally simple tricks for maintaining and repairing PCs. There's nothing in here that requires you to whip out a soldering gun, strip wires, or run expensive diagnostic equipment.

The advice here comes from years of scenarios like the ones above and from tips I've received from others who, either through necessity or curiosity, have done their own repairs. Of course, the best advice is to avoid having to make any repairs in the first place. Chapter 16 is devoted to telling you the easy steps you can take to keep your computer in top shape. But since the best-laid prevention isn't always enough, Chapter 17 covers the 12 steps to take to fix the most common malfunctions, plus the emergency procedure in case you douse your keyboard in coffee.

Of course, I hope you never have to use them. And the chances are excellent you won't. The PCs made today are about as stable a machine as you can get, despite how it may seem when something does go wrong. The components are seasoned veterans of whatever mishandling inevitably comes their way. At the worse, fixing a PC rarely means more than replacing some relatively inexpensive component. Often it doesn't even require a trip to the computer store.

Read the next couple of chapters now so you're aware generally of what you can do yourself to avoid calamity. Don't feel you have to memorize anything. Just know that these instructions are here, waiting to help, should disaster ever strike.

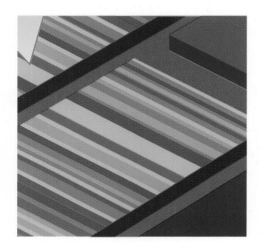

Computer Maintenance

THE MOST HIGH-STRUNG personal computer takes less maintenance than the average car. And you don't get your hands greasy. But just as an oil change doesn't do any good if you don't have it done every 3,000 miles, computer maintenance is useless if you don't do it on a regular basis.

I'm not going to suggest some daily regimen that even I wouldn't follow. Most of the tasks discussed here rarely need to be done more than once a month or even every six months. You can work many of them into your regular schedule. While you're at lunch is a good time to run a disk maintenance program. Myself, I have a tendency to procrastinate as a writer when it comes to deadlines. But I've been able to turn this vice to a virtue by discovering maintenance procedures that I simply must take care of immediately, instead of working on that overdue chapter.

If you've followed the advice in Chapters 3 and 4 about setting up your PC properly in the first place, creating a floppy boot disk and making hard copy records of your CMOS set-up screens, then you've already done the most important steps of emergency planning. But there are a few other procedures that can help you avoid having to read the following chapter—which discusses how to take care of a PC *after* something's gone wrong. Learning to control heat and take care of your hard drives now will help you prevent breakdowns later.

The great enemy of computers is heat—well, not exactly heat, but changes in temperature. All computer components generate heat and all are designed to withstand some amount of fluctuation in temperature. But there's a limit to how much and how often a PC component can go from cold to over 100° F without bad side effects. Like anything else, when a computer component—a chip, a circuit board, a connector—gets warmer, it expands. As it cools, it contracts. What this hot-cold movement can do is make chips and expansion cards creep out of their sockets, crack electrical traces on circuit boards, and break solder joints. In rare cases, heating and rapid cooling can cause condensation on hard-drive platters. Here's one plan for beating the heat: Never turn off your computer. That's maybe a bit too much to ask. But in theory, never turning off your PC—so that it never has a chance to cool off—would eliminate most of the damage caused by fluctuating temperature. In reality, leaving on your PC constantly may be impractical. It draws power, and that's expensive—although new "green" PCs are built to go into a power-saving mode if they're left inactive for several minutes. There is a real fire hazard danger; monitors have been known to short and start fires. And an unattended computer turned on is a security risk.

A reasonable alternative to keeping your computer turned on permanently is turning off your computer only once a day. If you leave for lunch or an hour meeting, or if someone else is going to use the same computer after you, leave it on. Not only does this reduce the number of times the PC heats and cools, it reduces that crucial time—start-up—at which a PC or peripheral is most likely to crack under pressure. Think back to when you've had light bulbs burn out. Most of the burn-outs happened when you turned on the lights—right? The same kind of stress that can overwhelm a light bulb at the moment it's turned on can also plague a computer when you flip its on switch. When you turn on a PC, several components demand electricity at once, and some, such as hard drives, need more power to get started than they do when running at full speed. The surges of electricity can be the final straw for a component that has only a marginal grip on life.

If you're concerned about someone snooping around a computer you've left on and unattended, use a screen saver. Most have password-protection features that stop others from accessing your private files. And by blanking the screen, the saver makes your monitor use less electricity. I'm not sure it's significantly less, but why overlook a chance to be green?

And, by the way, don't think you can make your PC run cooler by removing the cover. Most PCs' cabinets are designed for forced-air draw-through by the computer fan so that the air circulates over the components most suspectible to overheating—such as the microprocessor. Plus, the case protects the components from an even heavier blanket of dust than they accumulate with the cover in place.

In addition to controlling heat, you need to take care of your hard drive. Your hard drive is the most untiring component you have. The platters inside it are spinning at thousands of revolutions a minute all the time your PC is on—not just when you read or write data. And it's a sealed component. You can't open it up to give it a drop of oil or somehow relieve its drugery. But you can ease its work load, increase its performance, and better ensure the integrity of the information you've stored on it. The way to accomplish this is with two procedures: defragmentation and a surface scan.

Disk files are fragmented because of the way DOS saves files. Initially files are written in long continuous *clusters*, made up of sectors of a track. But in the normal course of events, files are erased, leaving holes of unused clusters among clusters reserved for files. As a new file is saved, it may be divided into several portions that are spread among the holes of unused files. Such a file is *fragmented*; that is, scattered throughout widely separated parts of the hard drive. Because the read/write heads have to move around more when they are retrieving or writing the file, the process takes longer and wears out the mechanisms sooner.

A defragmenter utility program, such as the DEFRAG that comes with MS-DOS 6, corrects the problem by juggling those fragments among unused parts of the disk until all the parts of each file are contiguous. Use DEFRAG or any of the similar programs, such as Norton Utilities Speed Disk, about once every week to once a month. Most programs let you check first to find out what percentage of the disk is fragmented. If the percentage of free disk space plus the percentage of the files that are fragmented rise above 20 percent of the disk size, run a defragging program. The more often you run it, the less time it takes.

All hard disk platters are imperfect. Although the ideal is a perfectly smooth recording surface that's exactly the same thickness everywhere, the reality is different. The magnetic coating may vary in thickness, and natural pits in the surface can become worse as they're tugged and pulled by the spinning disk's enormous centrifugal force and by the tidal currents of magnetic fields.

Although a defect might not be so gross that data couldn't be written to it at one time, the defect can erode to the point that its data cannot be read. A program such as Norton Utilities Disk Doctor or ScanDisk in DOS 6.2 meticulously writes test data to every sector on a hard drive and attempts to read it back. The data in any sectors that the utility has difficulty reading are moved to known good sectors, and the defective sectors are marked as bad in a table used by DOS to keep track of files. DOS then will not attempt to write data to the bad sectors in the future.

The final precaution to take for disk protection is to scan regularly with an antivirus utility. Computer viruses are like UFO abductions. People don't take them seriously unless they're the ones riding off to Alpha Centauri or to a disk crash. I've discovered one virus on my system. It was harmless and easy to get rid of, but it was still enough to make me a believer.

A virus checker is a program that inspects files for tell-tale signs of a virus infection or a computer operation that's typical of virus mischief. The program notifies the user, who often can then use an eradication program to stamp out the virus. Most programs, including the ones supplied with different versions of DOS, can catch most viruses. But I prefer Dr. Solomon's Anti-Virus Toolkit.

Run a virus checker daily if you are frequently exchanging data or floppy disks with others. Run it weekly if you only do the occasional download of a file from a bulletin board. Run it at least once a month unless you're a hermit.

Battling Dirt and Dust

Besides heat, the next greatest enemy of your PC is dust. When dust builds up on chips and circuits, it acts as a blanket, holding in the heat that the components generate. Dust and dirt can also contain chemical contaminants that conduct electricity. They may be microscopic to our eye but they are rivers of electricity on the scale of computer circuits. They can cause an electrical short or change the logic of a circuit by creating a signal where there should be none. In battling dust—and heat—your best ally is canned air. Adjust the following dusting schedule to your own situation. In a controlled-climate office, this schedule is about right. But if you work with the windows open or in a generally dustier environment, you should take these steps more often.

Chip

Dust

Once a month

1 Turn off and unplug your PC, and ground yourself to prevent static discharges. Then remove the case from your PC.

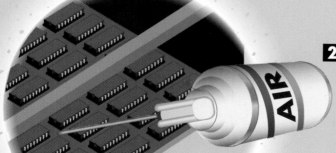

2 Direct canned air at the motherboard from different angles to get dust that may accumulate in hidden pockets.

3 Spray both sides of expansion boards. You can use foam rubber swabs to loosen accumulations of debris on expansion boards and the motherboard before blasting it with air. But don't use brushes, cotton swabs, or pieces of cloth. They can produce static charges and leave their own residue.

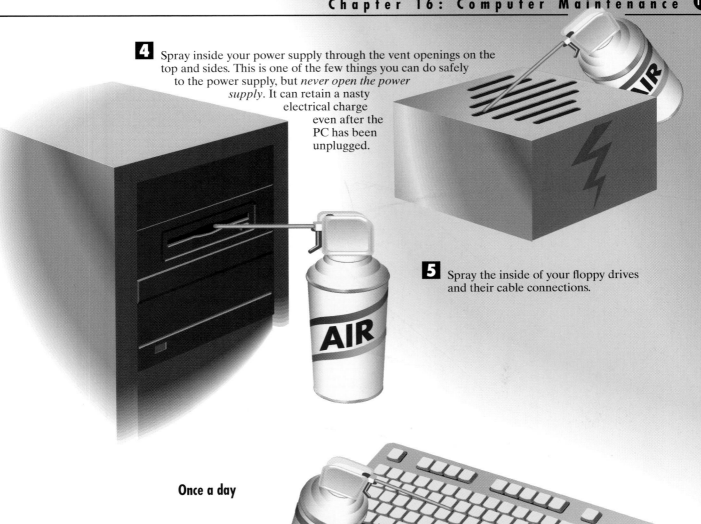

4 Spray inside your power supply through the vent openings on the top and sides. This is one of the few things you can do safely to the power supply, but *never open the power supply*. It can retain a nasty electrical charge even after the PC has been unplugged.

5 Spray the inside of your floppy drives and their cable connections.

Once a day

Use canned air in the openings that surround the keys in your keyboard. Over time you'll see bits of paper, balls of dusts, cookie crumbs, and bugs—the organic kind, not silicon ones—fly out of the keyboard. About once a week as you spray it, turn the keyboard upside down to encourage trapped bits to exit.

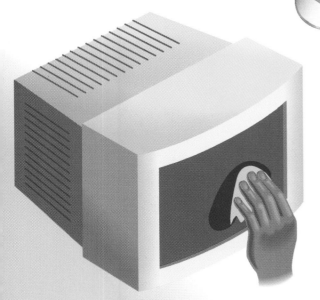

On the monitor's screen, use a screen cleaner, preferably one that counters static buildup. Ordinary household glass cleaners don't do as good a job as the specialized products, and they may dissolve screen coatings. If you can't find screen cleaner, use isopropyl alcohol rather than glass cleaner. Proper cleaning will not only make your screen brighter and sharper, but it removes a static charge that causes dust to cling to the screen; this dust can then make its way to other parts of your PC.

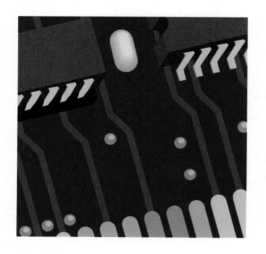

CHAPTER 17

The Midnight Drill

WHEN I GOT my first personal computer in 1981, no one knew that much about them. I soon learned that the dealer I bought it from didn't either. And the one time I sent it in for repairs under the warranty, it took nearly a month until it was returned. When I finally got it back, not only was the problem not fixed, but one of the floppy drives was dangling loose in its bay and screws were missing.

My only constant sources of information were computer magazines and a local users group, made up mostly of people like me hoping to swap tips and secrets with others. If you don't belong to a users group, join one today. Large users groups provide classes, purchase discounts, inexpensive shareware, and electronic bulletin boards. Even small groups at least give you the opportunity to meet with others to exchange computing war stories. You can easily earn back a users group's annual dues with one piece of advice that saves you a repair bill.

Another source of advice is a major information network such as ZiffNet, Interchange Online Network, CompuServe, Prodigy, or America Online. Every question that I've left on these services has always received a reply. Sometimes the person giving me advice was a programmer who worked on the software that I'm having problems with. That's as authoritative as you can get. Exploring these on-line services can be as expensive as it is fascinating, but a few strategically placed questions can make the service pay for itself.

Anyway, besides computer magazines, a users group, and on-line services, I've been pretty much on my own when it comes to fixing PCs. I've made some mistakes. (Do not use WD-40 spray to try to unstick a sticky keyboard. Trust me.) I've had to resort to a repair shop only two or three times in more than a decade. Most of the time I've been able, on my own, to fix the problem, or at least narrow it down to a single part I needed to replace. By doing that I've come up with the 12 tips on the next pages to follow anytime your PC starts acting up or playing dead. I've found that these tips remedy whatever's wrong about 90 percent of the time. I call them the Midnight Drill because it seems that, inevitably, I need to follow them late at night when I can't even call some user group guru for advice.

A lot of these procedures involve turning off your PC, changing something, and then turning it on again to see what happens. Because I don't want to repeat the same warning each time (and you'd get tired of reading it), I want to say very emphatically right now, *before you open up your computer to work inside it, touch the metal case to discharge any static that's built up in your body; then make sure your PC is turned off and unplugged before tinkering with the inside of it. That applies to all the tips and to all the advice throughout this book.*

If you take those precautions, the worst that any of the following suggestions can do is not solve the problem. But you don't have to worry about making the situation worse. And nine times out of ten, the tips will help you fix your PC, or at least keep it going long enough to get you through the night.

The 12-Step Midnight Drill

It's one of those rules of life that disaster strikes at the exact moment you're least prepared for it. The TV blacks out during the Superbowl. The
car conks out on vacation. The PC goes on the fritz
when you need it to meet a deadline at the office,
never when you're just playing Flight Simulator.

1 **Don't panic.** If you're already tense when a computer problem happens, you'll only make the situation worse if you get
more emotional. That's why when something serious goes
wrong, particularly on deadline, the first thing you should do
is—anything else. Walk the dog. Watch five minutes of televi-
sion while you drink something decaffeinated. Get a snack.
You'll calm down and then you can follow the rest of these
suggestions without randomly tearing apart your computer. I
speak from experience. A couple of times I've panicked and
had my system half disassembled before the adrenaline ran
out and I gathered my wits about me. Each time the solution
was a simple one that I would have spotted much quicker if I
hadn't let my fears take over.

2 **Hope for a miracle.** There are a lot of unex-
plained mysteries in computing. Something will
go wrong, but if you turn everything off and then
reboot, the problem has disappeared. It's a miracle. You'll never get the problem to reproduce itself so that you can fix it permanently. And that's
fine. You may lose whatever work you haven't
saved to disk so far, but hitting the off/on switch
is the fastest fix for a system that is producing a
lot of garbage on screen or that refuses to do anything at all but beep annnoyingly.

3 **Narrow down the problem.** Although it may seem like it at times, it's not your entire PC that's causing you trouble. It's just one specific component. Try to determine the exact source of the problem. For example, you may not be able to print a document. The problem could be caused by your software, the printer, cabling from the PC to the printer, or by how Windows is set up. Check your printer for error messages and try turning it off and on. If you're in Windows, try to print from another Windows application. Exit Windows and see if you can print from a DOS application. The results of each of these steps will point you further in the direction of the problem. A systematic way of narrowing down the problem includes the following steps:

Software or hardware? Most computer problems are caused by software bugs and memory conflicts. Eliminate software as a possibility by testing your PC with different programs before you start looking at hardware for the glitch.

What components are likely to be associated with the problem? If your screen is scrambled, the likely hardware suspects are your monitor and the video adapter. A hard-drive error could be caused by the drive itself or the drive controller card.

Swap components and see if the problem persists. There is a good reason not to throw out or sell old equipment. After you've bought an expensive Windows accelerator video adapter, you may think you no longer have a need for that old VGA card. But if you have display problems, taking out the new adapter and slipping in the old one can quickly tell you if the problem's in the newer card. Ideally, you should have as backup one of each type of cable on your system, a fresh CMOS battery, and one or two memory chips or SIMMs. When you upgrade, keep an old monitor, any working adapter cards, an outdated modem or printer. Each can help you track down a problem or could be the short-term solution until you get a permanent fix.

Review recent changes you've made to the system. All the effects of installing a new board or hardware drivers don't always show up immediately. You may install a new sound card, and it's only weeks later when you try to print at the same time that a sound file is being played that something screwy happens. Anytime a new piece of hardware or software requires changes in the CONFIG.SYS or AUTOEXEC.BAT files, you're leaving yourself open for a resource or memory conflict. That's why you should always back up those two files before installing any new hardware or software. You should also back up WIN.INI and SYSTEM.INI before installing new Windows software, fonts, or drivers. Even if some change in the last week or two doesn't appear to be a likely culprit, undo the changes—remove the new card or restore the original startup or .INI files—and see if the problem goes away. [*Continued on the next page.*]

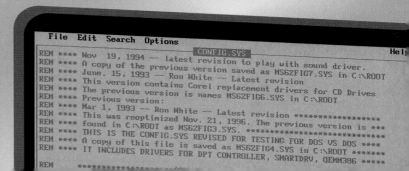

The 12-Step Midnight Drill

4 **Pay attention to your PC during boot-up.** The message displayed on screen as your PC performs its power-on self-test and as it loads drivers and programs from your CONFIG.SYS and AUTOEXEC.BAT files can often identify the source of a problem. But because the messages sometimes scroll by too fast to read, do this when you reboot: As soon as the message "Starting MS-DOS…" appears, press **F5**. Then for each line in your two start-up files, your PC will ask you to press **Y** or **N** before executing that line. Then you can see the results before executing the next line. Listen, too, to your PC during boot-up. The type of beeps it makes can give you information in a situation where some major hardware component is malfunctioning and you can't use other troubleshooting techniques. The chart here shows the meaning for various beep combinations. Check your PC's manual in case it differs.

Beeps (• = short, — = long)	Display	Problem Area
None	None	Power
None	Cursor only	Power
None	DOS prompt	Speaker
•	DOS prompt	Normal; no problem
•	BASIC screen (IBM only)	Disk
• —	None	Monitor/display adapter
• •	None	Monitor/display adapter
• •	Error code	Other, usually memory
Several •	305 error code	Keyboard
Several •	Anything else	Power
Continuous beep	Anything else	Power
— •	Anything else	System board
— • •	Anything else	Monitor/display adapter
— • • •	Anything else	Monitor/display adapter

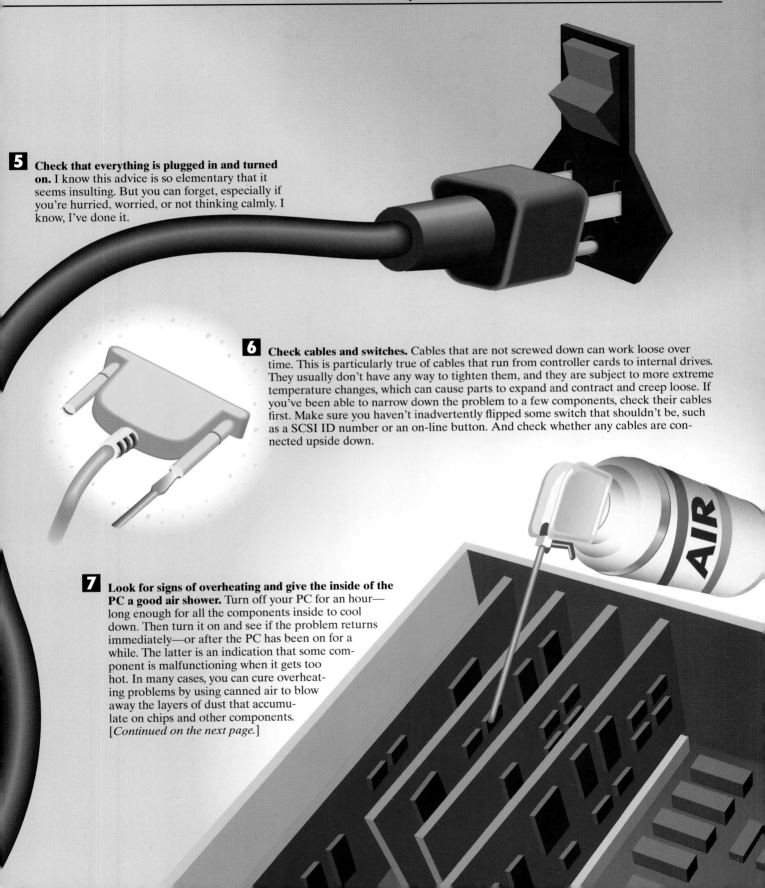

5 **Check that everything is plugged in and turned on.** I know this advice is so elementary that it seems insulting. But you can forget, especially if you're hurried, worried, or not thinking calmly. I know, I've done it.

6 **Check cables and switches.** Cables that are not screwed down can work loose over time. This is particularly true of cables that run from controller cards to internal drives. They usually don't have any way to tighten them, and they are subject to more extreme temperature changes, which can cause parts to expand and contract and creep loose. If you've been able to narrow down the problem to a few components, check their cables first. Make sure you haven't inadvertently flipped some switch that shouldn't be, such as a SCSI ID number or an on-line button. And check whether any cables are connected upside down.

7 **Look for signs of overheating and give the inside of the PC a good air shower.** Turn off your PC for an hour—long enough for all the components inside to cool down. Then turn it on and see if the problem returns immediately—or after the PC has been on for a while. The latter is an indication that some component is malfunctioning when it gets too hot. In many cases, you can cure overheating problems by using canned air to blow away the layers of dust that accumulate on chips and other components. [*Continued on the next page.*]

The 12-Step Midnight Drill

8 **Clean all contacts and reseat expansion boards.**
Although your expansion boards may be locked
down with a screw, temperature changes can make
them creep out of their sockets enough to cause at
least intermittent problems. And depending on the
quality of the gold plating on their contacts, corrosion may be interfering with a board's signals to the
bus. Use an unlubricated contact cleaner to bath the
contacts. Do not use cotton swabs; they leave cotton
fibers behind. Instead, use foam-rubber swaps available
at computer stores and electronics supply houses or lint-
free swabs that are already saturated with contact
cleaner. Some technicians recommend lubricated contact
cleaner because it makes it easier to insert the boards into
the slots, but I caution against the lubricated cleaner because it also makes it easier for the boards to work free, and
the lubricant can contain an oil that becomes gummy and
collects dust and contaminants. You should also clean the expansion slots and the cable connectors where they are attached to
the expansion boards, drives, and other devices. If the connection
from the power supply to the motherboard is removable, clean
those contacts also. (You may sometimes hear advice to clean the
contacts with an eraser. If this is really an emergency and you don't
have contact cleaner, then use the eraser. But be gentle. The coating of gold on the contacts is thin and if you rub it off, you expose
the underlying tin plating, which is highly susceptible to corrosion.)

Socketed chip   Surface-mounted chip

9 **Reseat socketed chips.** While you have the expansion boards
out, check all socketed chips on the motherboard and the expansion boards. Some chips are *surface-mounted*—their
leads are soldered directly to traces in the circuit board. But
other chips are *socketed*—they plug into sockets that, in
turn, are soldered to the board. Socketed chips are subject to
the same creeping disconnect process that heat changes
bring to other components. Make sure each socketed chip—
even if it appears to be in all the way—is fully seated by
pressing down on it firmly. But at the same time, make sure
that the board is supported from the other side, either by
your hand or by spacers that hold the motherboard away
from the PC's case. While pressing in the chips, you don't
want to bend the expansion boards or motherboard and risk
cracking them. After checking the chips and cleaning the expansion board and cable contacts, reseat the boards, making
sure they are inserted all the way and screwed down tightly.

10 **Look for sources of radio and electrical interference.** The stranger the problem with your system, the more you should suspect some sort of radio electrical interference from other electronic equipment or from other components in your computer system. For weeks once I was plagued by a Windows pointer that frequently took on a life of its own, scooting about the screen without me so much as touching the mouse. The problem turned out to be an electronic toy next to the monitor, which displayed a high-voltage spark that traveled along the inside of a glass globe. When I moved the globe a few more inches away from my PC, the pointer returned to normal. Interference can also be hidden within walls. For example, high-voltage lines running through the walls could affect the colors of your display. The fix could be to move the monitor away from the wall. Sometimes you can't move your system away from the interference because it is coming from your system components—say, the cable from your video card to the monitor. In those instances, purchase from an electrical supply store a *toroidal iron core*—two pieces of iron that snap together around a cable and cushion the cable from interference.

Toroidal iron core

11 **Relieve an overloaded power supply.** If you've crammed your PC so that each drive bay and expansion slot is filled, you could be pulling more electricity than your power supply can handle. If, when you boot your PC, the proper drive and panel lights come on, you know you're getting power. But if you hear any of the beeping patterns covered in step 4, and particularly if you hear a clicking sound before your PC fails, your power supply may not be strong enough to handle everything. Remove the power cables from any components that aren't absolutely necessary—such as both floppy drives and any second hard drive or internal CD-ROM drive. And remove adapter cards, such as sound cards and internal modems, that aren't essential. This isn't a permanent fix. It's designed only to bring down the power draw long enough to boot your system and at least copy some crucial data files to floppy. The power supply should be replaced with a bigger one, but this is a job you should leave to professionals.

12 **Replace the CMOS battery.** When your PC boots, it sends out signals to test for the presence of certain types of hardware. Then it compares what it finds with the hardware described in a CMOS memory chip. Its information comes from answers provided on the PC's setup screens. The CMOS memory retains the information while the computer is turned off, because the CMOS has its own small battery to keep the data alive. If the battery dies, your PC will boot to say you don't have a hard drive or will give you another message indicating that the CMOS information is wrong. A few batteries are soldered to the motherboard, and unless you're a lot better with a soldering gun than I am, you should get a dealer or repair shop to add a new battery. (And ask if you can have a battery holder rigged up that doesn't require soldering. You may have to change a jumper if you do this. Check your manual.) But if the battery is only clipped in or screwed down, you can do the swap yourself. The size, appearance, and location of batteries vary widely. Check the manual that came with your PC to find the battery and how to replace it.

Rescuing a Drowning Keyboard

There is nothing worse that you can do to your PC—and nothing you are as likely to do—than spill a sugared drink on your keyboard. You should be ashamed. And so should I. I've done this enough that I have a shelf full of dead keyboards. But at least they gave their lives helping me figure out what to do to minimize damage when Coke strikes.

Liquid itself isn't what damages your keyboard. It's the sugar and syrup in soft drinks and the sugar we add to coffee and tea. When the liquid evaporates, it leaves behind gummy sugar, which causes keys to stick. Of course, unsweetened tea and coffee can leave behind other residue, and you should clean up after any spill, but sugar is the main culprit. Here's what to do when any drink—sweet or not—gives your keyboard a bath.

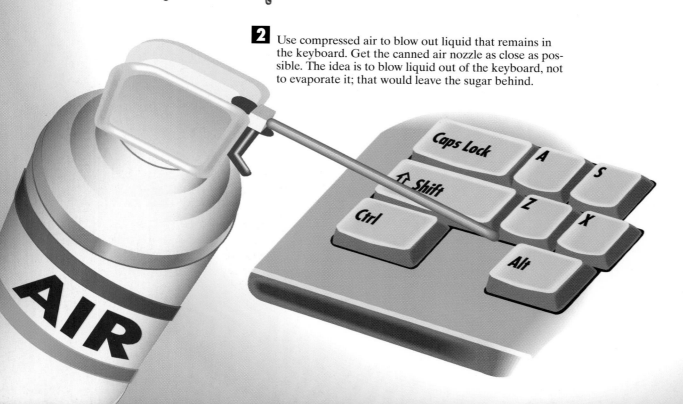

1 Immediately turn over the keyboard and shake it to get out as much liquid as possible.

2 Use compressed air to blow out liquid that remains in the keyboard. Get the canned air nozzle as close as possible. The idea is to blow liquid out of the keyboard, not to evaporate it; that would leave the sugar behind.

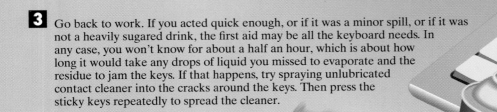

3 Go back to work. If you acted quick enough, or if it was a minor spill, or if it was not a heavily sugared drink, the first aid may be all the keyboard needs. In any case, you won't know for about a half an hour, which is about how long it would take any drops of liquid you missed to evaporate and the residue to jam the keys. If that happens, try spraying unlubricated contact cleaner into the cracks around the keys. Then press the sticky keys repeatedly to spread the cleaner.

4 If the problem persists, use a screwdriver or a chip puller to remove the key cap from the sticking key mechanism.

5 Use foam-rubber swabs and contact cleaner to clean all surfaces of the key and the parts of the board surrounding it. Don't count on being able to see the residue. Concentrate on cleaning around moving parts.

6 Replace the key cap by pressing straight down on the key post.

Some keys may loosen up over time and others get stickier. You may eventually have to get a replacement keyboard, but in most situations after I've applied the steps here, I've been able to continue using the keyboard—at least until the next spill.

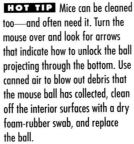

HOT TIP Mice can be cleaned too—and often need it. Turn the mouse over and look for arrows that indicate how to unlock the ball projecting through the bottom. Use canned air to blow out debris that the mouse ball has collected, clean off the interior surfaces with a dry foam-rubber swab, and replace the ball.

Default Settings for Popular Peripherals

Find the name of the adapter or device that you've installed or are thinking of installing at left and read across for default and alternative IRQ, base address, and DMA channel settings. If your device is not covered here, it may be configured similarly to one in its category, so you can at least get a feel for the potential pitfalls.

This material is courtesy of *PC/Computing*.

CD-ROM Drives

Device or Board	Default IRQ	Alternate IRQ	Default Base Address	Alternate Base Address	DMA Channel (Alternate)	Potential Device Conflicts	Technical Support
NEC CDR-74	N/A	N/A	CC00	C800, DC00, D800	1[3]	HD, NET, SCSI	(800) 338-8888, (508) 635-4000
Toshiba XM-3301	4[1]	3	CA00	C800, CE00, DE00	1[3]	COM2-4, HD, LPT2, NET, SCSI	(714) 455-0407
Sony CDU-6100, 6101, 6110, 6111, 6211, 7205, 7211[1]	N/A	2,3,4,5	0340	0300 through 03F0	1[3]	B, COM1-2	(800) 326-9551, (408) 894-0555
Sony CDU-541[1]	5[1]	3	CA00	C800, CE00, DE00	N/A	B, COM1-2	(800) 326-9551, (408) 894-0555
Sony CDU-510[1]	4[1,2]	N/A	0340	0300 through 03F0	1	B, COM1-2	(800) 326-9551, (408) 894-0555

(1) DOS software doesn't use an interrupt for CD-ROM drives.
(2) Interrupt setting is not required on AT and higher systems. Leaving interrupt settings at 4 will not interfere with other devices.
(3) XT-class PCs require setting of DMA 1.

N/A=Not applicable, which means that the device is either external or doesn't use that resource. In columns labeled alternate settings, where the device listed has a default setting, N/A means that no alternate setting is available.

Legend for Potential Device Conflicts B=Bus devices, EMS=EMS boards, FAX=Fax boards, F/M=Fax modem, HD=Hard drive, M=Modem, MC=Math coprocessor, NET=Network adapter, RTC=Real time clock, S=Sound cards, SCSI=SCSI devices, SCAN=Scanner, SERIAL=Serial port devices, SP=Serial printer, TBD=Tape backup drive, V=Video card

Hard Drive/Floppy Drive Adapters

Device or Board	Default IRQ	Alternate IRQ	Default Base Address	Alternate Base Address	DMA Channel (Alternate)	Potential Device Conflicts	Technical Support
Adaptec 1520, 1522	11	9,10,12	C800	CC00,D800,DC00	0	NET	(800) 959-7274, (408) 945-2550
Adaptec 1540B, 1542B	11	9,10,12,14,15	DC00	CC00,C800,D800	5	NET	(800) 959-7274, (408) 945-2550
Adaptec 1540C, 1542C	11	9,10,12,14	DC00	C800,CC00,D000, D400,D800,DC00	5	NET	(800) 959-7274, (408) 945-2550
Boca IDE Plus	7,4,3	2,5	N/A	N/A	N/A	COM1−2, NET, TBD,	(407) 241-8088
DTK or Clone IDE/IO (Model UN-1072)	7,4,3	2,5	N/A	N/A	N/A	COM1−2, NET, TBD,	(818) 810-8880
DPT SmartCache Plus SK2011/90	14	12,15	C800	D800,DC00	5	NET, TBD	(407) 830-5522
DPT SmartCache Plus SK2012/B	N/A	N/A	C800	D800	N/A	NET, TBD	(407) 830-5522
Western Digital WD1003 ST506 412	6	N/A	N/A	N/A	2	N/A	(714) 932-5000
Western Digital WD1006M ST506 412	6	N/A	N/A	N/A	2	N/A	(714) 932-5000
Western Digital WD1006V ST506 412	6	N/A	CC00	N/A	2	N/A	(714) 932-5000
UltraStor Ultra15C Caching IDE	14	15	D800	C800,CC00,D000, D400,DC00	N/A	NET, TBD, V	(510) 623-8955

I/O Cards

Device or Board	Default IRQ	Alternate IRQ	Default Base Address	Alternate Base Address	DMA Channel (Alternate)	Potential Device Conflicts	Technical Support
Boca I/O 2 by 4, IOAT41, IOAT42	7, 4, 3	2, 5	0378, 03F8, 02F8	0278, 03E8, 02E8	N/A	COM3—4, LPT2, RTC	(407) 241-8088
Boca I/OAT44	7,5,4,3	2	0378, 0278,03E8, 02E8	03E8, 02E8	N/A	COM3—4, RTC	(407) 241-8088
Everex Magic I/O (EV170 and EV170a)	5, 4, 3	2	0378, 03F8, 02F8	03BC, 0278	N/A	COM3—4, LPT1, RTC	(510) 498-1111
Modular Circuit Technology (JDR) MCT-AIO, MCT-A10+	7,5,4,3	2	0378, 0278, 03F8, 02F8	03BC, 0278	N/A	COM3—4, RTC	(408) 559-1200

Mice

Device or Board	Default IRQ	Alternate IRQ	Default Base Address	Alternate Base Address	DMA Channel (Alternate)	Potential Device Conflicts	Technical Support
Logitech Serial	4 (COM1, COM3)	3 (COM 2, COM 4)	03F8 (COM1)	02F8 (COM 2), 03E8 (COM3), 02E8 (COM4)	N/A	M, SP (COM3—4 where supported)	(510) 795-8100, (415) 795-0427
Logitech Bus	2	3,4,5	023C	0238	N/A	HD, LPT2, M, NET, SP, Video	(510) 795-8100, (415) 795-0427
Microsoft Serial	4 (COM1, COM3)	3 (COM 2, COM 4)	03F8 (COM1)	02F8 (COM 2), 03E8 (COM3), 02E8 (COM4)	N/A	M, SP (COM3—4 where supported)	(206) 637-7096
Microsoft Bus	2	3,4,5	023C	0238	N/A	LPT2, M, SP	(206) 637-7096
Mouse Systems Serial Card	4 (COM1, COM3)	3 (COM 2, COM 4)	03F8 (COM1)	02F8 (COM 2), 03E8 (COM3), 02E8 (COM4)	N/A	M, SP (COM3—4 where supported)	(510) 656-1117

Modems

Device or Board	Default IRQ	Alternate IRQ	Default Base Address	Alternate Base Address	DMA Channel (Alternate)	Potential Device Conflicts	Technical Support
USRobotics Sportster 14,400/PC and 14,400/PC F[1]	3 (COM2)	4, 5,7	02F8	03F8, 03E8,02E8	N/A	SERIAL	(800) 982-5151, (708) 982-5151
USRobotics Courier/PC and Courier/PC F (HST, V.32)[1]	3 (COM2)	4,5,7	02F8	03F8, 03E8,02E8	N/A	SERIAL	(800) 982-5151, (708) 982-5151
Practical Peripherals 2400EFX	4 (COM1)	3	03F8	02F8,03E8,02E8	N/A	SERIAL	(805) 496-7707
Practical Peripherals 9600FX	4 (COM1)	3	03F8	02F8,03E8,02E8	N/A	SERIAL	(805) 496-7707
Practical Peripherals 14400FXSA	N/A	N/A	N/A	N/A	N/A	SERIAL	(805) 496-7707
Intel SatisFaxtion M[2,3]	Software setup	2,3,4,5	N/A	03F8,02F8,03E8, 02E8	1 or 3 (fax option)	SERIAL, V	(503) 629-7000
Intel Connection CoProcessor Fax	Software setup	N/A	N/A	02A0,02A8,0330, 0340	1 or 3	HD, SCAN, SERIAL, V	(503) 629-7000
Hayes Smartmodem 2400B	4 (COM1)	3(COM2)	03F8	02F8	N/A	SERIAL	(404) 441-1617
Hayes JT Fax 9600B	N/A	N/A	N/A	CC00-CF80	N/A	HD, SCAN, SERIAL, V	(404) 441-1617
Hayes Smartmodem Optima (24, 96, 144)	4 (COM1)	3 (COM2)	03F8	02F8	N/A	SERIAL	(404) 441-1617
SupraFaxModem	Software setup	2,3,4,5	N/A	03F8,02F8,03E8, 02E8	N/A	SERIAL, V	(503) 967-2440
Complete Modem Plus, Complete Modem Plus External	3 (COM4)	4	02E8	03F8,02F8,03E8	N/A	SERIAL	(408) 434-9600

(1) Modem comes with recommended switch settings for a variety of communications software.
(2) Intel's TESTCOM automates the configuration process for COM port and IRQ.
(3) Intel SatisFAXtion uses DMA channel 1 or 3 when the fax option is installed.

Network Adapters

Device or Board	Default IRQ	Alternate IRQ	Default Base Address	Alternate Base Address	DMA Channel (Alternate)	Potential Device Conflicts	Technical Support
Hercules Network Card Plus	2	2,3,5	0398	0310,0390,0318	3 (1,2)	COM2/4, LPT2, S, SCSI, SCAN, TBD	(510) 623-6030
Artisoft A2mbps	3	N/A	0280	0200–03E0	N/A	COM1/3, COM2/4, LPT1–2, S, SCSI, SCAN, TBD	(510) 623-6030
Artisoft AE-2 Ethernet	3	2,4–7,10,15	0300	0320,0340,0360	Disabled (1,3,5,7)	COM1/3, COM2/4, LPT1–2, S ,SCSI, SCAN, TBD	(510) 623-6030
Madge Smart 16/4 AT Ringnode	3	2–3,5,7, 9–12, 15	0A20	1A20,2A20,3A20	5 (1,2,4–6)	COM1/3, COM2/4, LPT1–2, S, SCSI, SCAN, TBD	(800) 876-2343
Madge Smart 16/4 MC Ringnode	Software setup	Software setup	Software setup	Software setup	Software setup	COM1/3, COM2/4, LPT1–2, S, SCSI, SCAN, TBD	(408) 955-0700
SMC/Western Digital Ethernet/10BASE-T	3	2,4–5,7, 10–12,15	0280	0320	N/A	COM1/3, COM2/4, LPT1–2, S, SCSI, SCAN, TBD	(714) 707-2200
Eagle Technology NE1000	3	2–5	0300	0320–0360	N/A	COM1/3, COM2/4, LPT1–2, S, SCSI, SCAN, TBD	(408) 745-0700
Eagle Technology NE2000	3	2,4,5	0300	0320–0360	N/A	COM1/3, COM2/4, LPT1–2, S, SCSI, SCAN, TBD	(800) 726-5267
Eagle Technology NE3200	3	4–5,9–11	0300	4000–9000, D000	N/A	COM1/3, COM2/4, LPT1–2, S ,SCSI, SCAN, TBD	(800) 726-5267
Intel EtherExpress 16 and 16TP (old models)	3	2,4–5,9–11	0300	0310–0370	N/A	COM1/3, COM2/4, LPT1–2, S, SCSI, SCAN, TBD	(503) 629-7000
Intel EtherExpress 16, 16TP, and 16C	3	2,4–5,9–11	0300	0310–0370	N/A	COM1/3, COM2/4, LPT1–2, S, SCSI, SCAN, TBD	(503) 629-7000

Network Adapters (Continued)

Device or Board	Default IRQ	Alternate IRQ	Default Base Address	Alternate Base Address	DMA Channel (Alternate)	Potential Device Conflicts	Technical Support
Proteon ProNet-4/16	3	2,4–5,9–11	0300	0310–0370	N/A	COM1/3, COM2/4, LPT1–2, S, SCSI, SCAN, TBD	(508) 898-3100
Thomas Conrad TC5045 Ethernet/AT[1]	3	2,5,7,9–12,15	0300	0100–0160, 0320–0340	5 (1,6,7)	COM1/3, COM2/4, LPT1–2,S, SCSI, SCAN, TBD	(800) 332-8683
Thomas Conrad TC5143 Ethernet/AT[1]	3	2,5,7,9–12,15	0300	0100–0160, 0320–0340	5 (1,6,7)	COM1/3, COM2/4, LPT1–2, S, SCSI, SCAN, TBD	(512) 836-1935

(1) Setup software can help automate the jumper settings before the adapter has been installed.

RAM Cards

Device or Board	Default IRQ	Alternate IRQ	Default Base Address	Alternate Base Address	DMA Channel (Alternate)	Potential Device Conflicts	Technical Support
BocaRAM 8-bit[1]	D000[4]	E000[4]	0268	0208,0218,0258	N/A	NET, V	(407) 241-8088
BocaRAM AT[1]	D000[4]	A000[4]	0268	0208,0218,0258	N/A	NET, V	(407) 241-8088
BocaRAM/AT Plus (SIMM) version[2]	N/A	N/A	N/A	N/A	N/A	NET, V	(407) 241-8088
BocaRAM/AT Plus (DRAM) version[2]	N/A	N/A	N/A	N/A	N/A	NET, V	(407) 241-8088
Orchid RamQuest 8/16	N/A	N/A	N/A	0208,0300,0308, 0310,0600,0608	N/A	NET, V	(510) 683-0323
Intel AboveBoard[3]	D000[4]	C000[4]	0370	0270,0350	N/A	HD, NET, V	(503) 629-7354

(1) Includes software LIM EMS 4.0 emulator driver.
(2) Boca recommends removing network adapter while configuring AT Plus card to avoid conflict at address 0300.
(3) The AboveBoard, set at A000 for the page frame in an IBM AT, can damage either the AboveBoard or the AT motherboard.
(4) Memory adapters don't use IRQs but take up an address in the expanded memory page frame if configured to use expanded memory.

Scanners

Device or Board	Default IRQ	Alternate IRQ	Default Base Address	Alternate Base Address	DMA Channel (Alternate)	Potential Device Conflicts	Technical Support
ScanPlus Plustek	N/A	N/A	0270	0220–0370	1 or 3	COM1–2, HD, LPT1–2, NET, S	(408) 980-1234
The Complete Page Scanner	2	3, 4, or 5	03E0	0220–03E0	1 or 3	COM1–2, HD, LPT 1–2, NET, S	(408) 434-9600
The Complete Half-Page Scanner	2	3, 4, or 5	03E0	0220–03E0	1 or 3	COM1–2, HD, LPT1–2, NET, S	(408) 434-9600
Logitech ScanMan 32, Logitech ScanMan 256	3[1]	2,4,5,7,9, 11–12	0280	02A0, 0330, 0340	1 or 3[1]	COM1–2, HD, LPT1–2, NET, S	(510) 795-8100
Logitech ScanMan Color	2[1]	2,4,5,7,9, 11–12	0280	02A0, 0330, 0340	1 or 3[1]	COM1–2, HD, LPT1–2, NET, S	(510) 795-8100
Hewlett-Packard ScanJet IIc	Software setup	Software setup	Software setup	C800–E400	Software setup	EMS Page Frame, HD, NET, S	(208) 323-2551
Intel Hand Scanner (SatisFaxtion)	2	3–5,7,10–11	0300	0320–03E0	1 or 3	COM1–2, HD, LPT1–2, NET, S, TBD	(503) 629-7354

(1) Older ScanMan controllers require hardware jumpers for IRQ and DMA channel. Newer controllers select the IRQ and DMA channel on the device's command line in CONFIG.SYS.

Sound Boards

Device or Board	Default IRQ	Alternate IRQ	Default Base Address	Alternate Base Address	DMA Channel (Alternate)	Potential Device Conflicts	Technical Support
Media Vision Pro AudioSpectrum 16[1,2,3,4,6]	7	2–4,6,10–12, 15	0220	0230, 0240	3 (0–2,5–7)	COM1–2, LPT1–2, NET, SCSI, SCAN, TBD	(800) 638-2807, (510) 770-9905
Media Vision Pro AudioSpectrum Plus[1,2,3,4,6]	7	2–4,6,10–12, 15	0220	0230, 0240	3 (0–2,5–7)	COM1–2, LPT1–2, NET, SCSI, SCAN, TBD	(800) 638-2807, (510) 770-9905
Microsoft Windows Sound System[5]	11	7, 9–10	0530	0604, 0E80, 0F40	0 (1,3)	Video, HD	(206) 635-7040

Sound Boards (Continued)

Device or Board	Default IRQ	Alternate IRQ	Default Base Address	Alternate Base Address	DMA Channel (Alternate)	Potential Device Conflicts	Technical Support
Creative Labs' Sound Blaster[6,7,9]	5	2, 3, 7	0220	0240	1 (0,3)	COM1−2, LPT1−2, NET, SCSI, SCAN, TBD	(408) 428-6622
Creative Labs' Sound Blaster Pro[6,7,9]	5	2, 3, 7, 10	0220	0240	1 (0,3)	COM1−2, LPT1−2, NET, SCSI, SCAN, TBD	(408) 428-6622
Creative Labs' Sound Blaster 16 ASP (Audio) [6,7,9]	5	2, 3, 7, 10	0220	0240	1 (0,3)	COM1−2, LPT1−2, NET, SCSI, SCAN, TBD	(408) 428-6622
>Creative Labs' Video Blaster[8]	10	5, 11, 12	2AD6	2A90, 2AF0	1	COM1−2, LPT1−2, NET, SCSI, SCAN, TBD	(408) 428-6622
Artisoft Lantastic Voice Adapter	Auto-configuring	Auto-configuring	Auto-configuring	Auto-configuring	1	COM1−2, LPT1−2, NET, SCSI, SCAN, TBD	(602) 293-6363

For sound cards, most DOS-based applications only recognize DMA1 and DMA3, and IRQs 2,3,5, and 7.

(1) Pro AudioSpectrum DMA and IRQ settings can be changed by altering the driver configuration in CONFIG.SYS. The IRQ and base address settings on the SoundBlaster section of the card must be changed by altering jumpers. The SoundBlaster section uses IRQ 5 and address 0220 as defaults.

(2) The software to drive the Pro AudioSpectrum products includes an installation utility to check the DMA and IRQ settings.

(3) Pro AudioSpectrum supports Chinon, Denon, Hitachi, IBM, Laser Magnetics, NEC, Panasonic, Pioneer, Sony, Texel, and Toshiba. Other SCSI devices are also supported (such as hard drives, and so on) with an add-on kit.

(4) Media Vision provides both internal and external SCSI cable/driver kits for $49 to $79, depending on the CD-ROM drive attached.

(5) Microsoft Sound System defaults to DMA channel 0 if board is installed in a 16-bit slot.

(6) Multiple Pro AudioSpectrum 16 boards can be installed by changing the board ID at jumper J2.

(7) SoundBlaster/SoundBlasterPro boards support only Panasonic/Matsushita CD-ROM drives.

(8) VideoBlaster can coreside with standard VGA cards through the feature connector.

(9) Nearly all SoundBlaster cards shipped before June 1, 1993, were shipped with the default IRQ set at IRQ7, a direct conflict with LPT1.

Tape Backup Drives

Device or Board	Default IRQ	Alternate IRQ	Default Base Address	Alternate Base Address	DMA Channel (Alternate)	Potential Device Conflicts	Technical Support
Mountain FileSafe-4440, TD-250 [2,3,4]	6	N/A	03E7	01E7	2	COM3−4, FAX, HD, LPT1−2, NET, SCAN	(408) 438-4897
Mountain FileSafe 1200	11	12	0330	0300,0370,03E0	5 [1]	COM3−4, FAX, HD, LPT1−2, NET, SCSI, SCAN	(408) 438-4897

Tape Backup Drives (Continued)

Device or Board	Default IRQ	Alternate IRQ	Default Base Address	Alternate Base Address	DMA Channel (Alternate)	Potential Device Conflicts	Technical Support
Mountain FileSafe 7000/ 7060/7150/7250	3	N/A	0288	028C	1	COM3—4, FAX, HD, LPT1—2, NET, SCAN	(408) 438-4897
Mountain FileSafe 8000Plus/TD4000, 8500IDE	6	N/A	03E7	01E7	2	COM3—4, FAX, HD, LPT1—2, NET, SCAN	(408) 438-4897
Colorado Jumbo 120, Trakker 120 [2,3]	N/A	N/A	N/A	N/A	N/A	COM3—4, FAX, HD, LPT1—2, NET, SCAN	(800) 845-7906, (303) 669-6500
Colorado Jumbo 250, Trakker 250 [2,3]	N/A	N/A	N/A	N/A	N/A	COM3—4, FAX, HD, LPT1—2, NET, SCAN	(800) 845-7906, (303) 669-6500
Colorado PowerTape 4000	N/A	N/A	N/A	N/A	N/A	COM3—4, FAX, HD, LPT1—2, NET, SCSI, SCAN	(800) 845-7906, (303) 669-6500
Maynard MaynStream 250 Q [1]	3	2,4—7	0370	0360	1 (2)	COM3—4, FAX, HD, LPT1—2, NET, SCSI, SCAN	(800) 227-6296, (407) 263-3500
Maynard MaynStream 525 Q [1]	3	2,4—7	0370	0360	1 (2)	COM3—4, FAX, HD, LPT1—2, NET, SCSI, SCAN	(800) 227-6296, (407) 263-3500
Maynard MaynStream 1350 Q	3	2,4—7	0370	0360	1 (2)	COM3—4, FAX, HD, LPT1—2, NET, SCSI, SCAN	(800) 227-6296, (407) 263-3500
Maynard MaynStream 2000 DAT [1]	3	2,4—7	0370	0360	1 (2)	COM3—4, FAX, HD, LPT1—2, NET, SCSI, SCAN	(800) 227-6296, (407) 263-3500
Maynard MaynStream 4000 DAT [1]	3	2,4—7	0370	0360	1 (2)	COM3—4, FAX, HD, LPT1—2, NET, SCSI, SCAN	(800) 227-6296, (407) 263-3500
Maynard MaynStream 2200 HS+	3	2,4—7	0370	0360	1 (2)	COM3—4, FAX, HD, LPT1—2, NET, SCSI, SCAN	(800) 227-6296, (407) 263-3500
Maynard MaynStream 5000 HS	3	2,4—7	0370	0360	1 (2)	COM3—4, FAX, HD, LPT1—2, NET, SCSI, SCAN	(800) 227-6296, (407) 263-3500

Tape Backup Drives (Continued)

Device or Board	Default IRQ	Alternate IRQ	Default Base Address	Alternate Base Address	DMA Channel (Alternate)	Potential Device Conflicts	Technical Support
Maynard Irwin EzPort	6	2–5,7	0370	03E0,03F0,0360	2 (1,4)	COM3–4, FAX, HD, LPT1–2, NET, SCSI, SCAN	(800) 227-6296, (407) 263-3500
Maynard AccuTrak (A120E), AccuTrak Plus (A250E)	N/A	N/A	N/A	N/A	N/A	COM3–4, FAX, HD, LPT1–2, NET, SCAN	(800) 227-6296, (407) 263-3500
Maynard Archive XL (ST250Q, 525Q, 1350Q, 2000, 4000) [2,3]	3	2,4–7	0370	0360	1 (2)	COM3–4, FAX, HD, LPT1–2, NET, SCAN	(800) 227-6296, (407) 263-3500
Iomega Bernoulli [1]	5	7	0340	0350-0368	3 (1)	COM3–4, FAX, HD, LPT1–2, NET, SCAN	(801) 778-3000

(1) If you already have a device using SCSI ID 0, select SCSI ID 2–6 for the tape drive.

(2) Can be installed as a third drive (in lieu of using a dedicated controller) with a three-drive cable. Your system may also require a power splitter.

(3) Some systems (PS/2, Compaq, and others) may require a proprietary controller.

(4) Mountain's MACH 2 controller uses IRQ2, DMA3, BASE 03E7. Alternate addresses via software setup.

Video*

Device or Board	Default IRQ	Alternate IRQ	Default Base Address	Alternate Base Address	DMA Channel (Alternate)	Potential Device Conflicts	Technical Support
Orchid Fahrenheit [1]	12	9–12 [2]	0344 [2]	0354	N/A	EMS, FAX, HD, NET, SCAN	(510) 683-0323
Orchid Fahrenheit 1280°, 1280°/D [1]	N/A	9	02E0 [1]	N/A	N/A	COM3–4, EMS, FAX, HD, NET, SCAN	(510) 683-0323
Orchid ProDesigner II	N/A	2	N/A	N/A	N/A	EMS, FAX, HD, NET, SCAN	(510) 683-0323
Orchid ProDesignerIIs	N/A	2	N/A	N/A	N/A	EMS, FAX, HD, NET, SCAN	(510) 683-0323
ATI Graphics Ultra, UltraPro, UltraPlus, Graphics Vantage	N/A	2,3,5	02E0 [1]	023C, 0238 (Bus mouse)	N/A	COM3–4, EMS, FAX, HD, NET, SCAN	(416) 756-0711

Video* (Continued)

Device or Board	Default IRQ	Alternate IRQ	Default Base Address	Alternate Base Address	DMA Channel (Alternate)	Potential Device Conflicts	Technical Support
ATI VGA Wonder XL	N/A	2,3,5	N/A	023C, 0238 (Bus mouse)	N/A	COM3–4, EMS, FAX, HD, NET, SCAN	(416) 756-0711
ATI 8514/Ultra [3]	N/A	2,3,5	N/A	N/A	N/A	COM3–4, EMS, FAX, HD, NET, SCAN	(416) 756-0711
ATI VGA Wonder	N/A	2,3,5	02E0 [1]	023C, 0238 (Bus mouse)	N/A	COM3–4, EMS, FAX, HD, NET, SCAN	(416) 756-0711
ATI VGA Wonder XL24	N/A	2,3,5	02E0 [1]	023C, 0238 (Bus mouse)	N/A	COM3–4, EMS, FAX, HD, NET, SCAN	(416) 756-0711
Matrox Impression Ultra	N/A	9	7C00	N/A	N/A	EMS, HD, NET, SCAN	(800) 462-8769, (514) 685-2630
Matrox Impression 1024	N/A	9	N/A	N/A	N/A	EMS, HD, NET, SCAN	(800) 462-8769, (514) 685-2630
Video Seven VRAM II Ergo	2	N/A	N/A	N/A	N/A	EMS, HD, NET, SCAN	(510) 656-7800
Video Seven VEGA VGA	2	N/A	N/A	N/A	N/A	EMS, HD, NET, SCAN	(510) 656-7800
Video Seven WIN.VGA	2	N/A	N/A	N/A	N/A	EMS, HD, NET, SCAN	(510) 656-7800
Video Seven 1024i Plus	2	N/A	N/A	N/A	N/A	EMS, HD, NET, SCAN	(510) 656-7800
Artist Graphics WinSprint 100+[1]	N/A	N/A	N/A	N/A	N/A	COM3–4, EMS, FAX, HD, NET, SCAN	(800) 627-8478, (612) 631-7800
Artist Graphics Xj1000[1]	N/A	N/A	03E0	02C0–02E0, 03C0,03F0	N/A	COM3–4, EMS, FAX, HD, NET, SCAN	(800) 627-8478, (612) 631-7800
Artist Graphics XJS[1]	N/A	N/A	03E0	02C0–02E0, 03C0,03F0	N/A	COM3–4, EMS, FAX, HD, NET, SCAN	(800) 627-8478, (612) 631-7800
Western Digital/Paradise SuperVGA	N/A	N/A	N/A	N/A	N/A	EMS, HD, NET, SCAN	(714) 932-4900
Western Digital/Paradise Accelerator Card for Windows	N/A	N/A	N/A	N/A	N/A	EMS, HD, NET, SCAN	(714) 932-4900
Boca Super VGA	N/A	N/A	N/A	N/A	N/A	EMS, HD, NET, SCAN	(407) 241-8088
Boca Super VGA Accelerated	N/A	N/A	N/A	N/A	N/A	EMS, HD, NET, SCAN	(407) 241-8088

Video* (Continued)

Device or Board	Default IRQ	Alternate IRQ	Default Base Address	Alternate Base Address	DMA Channel (Alternate)	Potential Device Conflicts	Technical Support
Boca Super VGA Brilliant Color	N/A	N/A	N/A	N/A	N/A	EMS, HD, NET, SCAN	(407) 241-8088
Boca Super X Accelerator VGA	N/A	N/A	N/A	N/A	N/A	EMS, HD, NET, SCAN	(407) 241-8088
Hercules VGA Card	N/A	N/A	N/A	N/A	N/A	EMS, HD, NET, SCAN	(510) 623-6030
Hercules Graphics Card	N/A	N/A	N/A	N/A	N/A	FAX, LPT1–2, SCAN	(510) 623-6030
Number Nine #9 GXE	N/A	N/A	N/A	N/A	N/A	EMS, HD, NET, SCAN	(617) 674-0009
Number Nine #9 GXiTC	N/A	N/A	02A0	0280,0290, 02B0–02E0	N/A	EMS, HD, NET, SCAN	(617) 674-0009
Sceptre VGA	2	5	N/A	N/A	N/A	EMS, HD, NET, SCAN	(408) 737-0888
STB PowerGraph X-24	N/A	2	N/A	02E8	N/A	COM3–4, EMS, FAX, HD, NET, SCAN	(214) 234-8750
Diamond Stealth 24	2	N/A	N/A	N/A	N/A	EMS, HD, NET, SCAN	(408) 736-2000

*With basic video boards, short of having to configure the adapter for a particular monitor, generally there are no IRQ and base address settings that need to be changed.

(1) May conflict with device on IRQ4, address 02E8.

(2) DMA channels 0 or 3, and IRQs 9–12 used for voice annotation option. Default DMA channel is 0.

(3) Combination card. Fits both ISA and MCA adapter slots.

DMAs (direct-memory-access channels), 73–74, 112

DOS drives, logical, 102–103

DOS partition, 102–103

DRAM (dynamic RAM), 37

drive bays, 17, 90

drivers, device. *See* device drivers

driver signature, 128

drives *See also* CD-ROM drives; hard drives; SCSI drives

  floppy, 16, 87

  form factor, 87

  installing, 87–93

  logical, 102–103

  mounting, 90–91

  types of, 87–89

  wiring, 92–93

drowning keyboard, rescuing, 150–151

Dr. Solomon's Anti-Virus Toolkit, 137

DSP (digital signal processor), 110

dual in-line package chips. *See* DIP chips

dust, battling, 138–139

dust-free location, selecting, 23

dynamic RAM. *See* DRAM

E

EISA (Extended Industry Standard Architecture), 59

EISA expansion slots, 59, 63, 65

EISA PCs, 74

electrical interference, 149

electrical outlets, grounded, 23

emergency, preparing for, 25–26, 28–31

emergency boot disk, making, 25–26, 31

emergency repairs, making, 133, 141–149

enhanced small device interface drives. *See* ESDI drives

error codes (DIP memory), translating, 44–47

error messages, bad memory, 41, 45

ESDI (enhanced small device interface)

  drives, 87–88

  installing, 96

  setting up, 98–99

expansion boards/cards/adapters, 12, 16, 57–81

  inserting, 70–71

  installing, 67–71

  inventory, 79

  removing, 68–69

  reseating, 148

  solving conflicts with, 73–74, 76–81

expansion buses, 58-59

  PCI, 60, 65

  VL, 59, 65

expansion slots, 16

  AT, 58

  EISA, 59, 63, 65

  ISA, 58, 63–64

  MCA, 64

  PC/XT, 64

  16-bit, 58

ATTENTION TEACHERS AND TRAINERS
Now You Can Teach From These Books!

ZD Press now offers instructors and trainers
the materials they need to use these books in their classes.

- An Instructor's Manual features flexible lessons designed for use in a 10- or 15-week course (30-45 course hours).

- Student exercises and tests on floppy disk provide you with an easy way to tailor and/or duplicate tests as you need them.

- A Transparency Package contains all the graphics from the book, each on a single, full-color transparency.

- Spanish edition of *PC/Computing How Computers Work* is available.

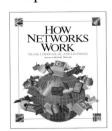

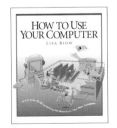
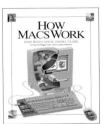

These materials are available only to qualified accounts. For more information contact:
Corporations, Government Agencies: Cindy Johnson, 800-488-8741, ext. 108
In the U.S.A: Academic Institutions: Suzanne Anthony, 800-786-6541, ext. 108
In Canada: Copp Clark Pitman Ltd.
In the U.K.: The Computer Bookshops
In Australia: WoodLane Pty. Ltd.

Ziff-Davis Press Survey of Readers

Please help us in our effort to produce the best books on personal computing.
For your assistance, we would be pleased to send you a FREE catalog
featuring the complete line of Ziff-Davis Press books.

1. How did you first learn about this book?

Recommended by a friend . . . . ☐ -1 (5)
Recommended by store personnel . . . . ☐ -2
Saw in Ziff-Davis Press catalog . . . . ☐ -3
Received advertisement in the mail . . . . ☐ -4
Saw the book on bookshelf at store . . . . ☐ -5
Read book review in: _____ ☐ -6
Saw an advertisement in: _____ ☐ -7
Other (Please specify): _____ ☐ -8

2. Which THREE of the following factors most influenced your decision to purchase this book? (Please check up to THREE.)

Front or back cover information on book . . .☐ -1 (6)
Logo of magazine affiliated with book . . . . . .☐ -2
Special approach to the content . . . .☐ -3
Completeness of content . . . .☐ -4
Author's reputation. . . . .☐ -5
Publisher's reputation . . . .☐ -6
Book cover design or layout . . . .☐ -7
Index or table of contents of book . . . .☐ -8
Price of book . . . .☐ -9
Special effects, graphics, illustrations . . . .☐ -0
Other (Please specify): _____ ☐ -x

3. How many computer books have you purchased in the last six months? _____ (7-10)

4. On a scale of 1 to 5, where 5 is excellent, 4 is above average, 3 is average, 2 is below average, and 1 is poor, please rate each of the following aspects of this book below. (Please circle your answer.)

Depth/completeness of coverage	5	4	3	2	1	(11)
Organization of material	5	4	3	2	1	(12)
Ease of finding topic	5	4	3	2	1	(13)
Special features/time saving tips	5	4	3	2	1	(14)
Appropriate level of writing	5	4	3	2	1	(15)
Usefulness of table of contents	5	4	3	2	1	(16)
Usefulness of index	5	4	3	2	1	(17)
Usefulness of accompanying disk	5	4	3	2	1	(18)
Usefulness of illustrations/graphics	5	4	3	2	1	(19)
Cover design and attractiveness	5	4	3	2	1	(20)
Overall design and layout of book	5	4	3	2	1	(21)
Overall satisfaction with book	5	4	3	2	1	(22)

5. Which of the following computer publications do you read regularly; that is, 3 out of 4 issues?

Byte . . . .☐ -1 (23)
Computer Shopper . . . .☐ -2
Corporate Computing . . . .☐ -3
Dr. Dobb's Journal . . . .☐ -4
LAN Magazine . . . .☐ -5
MacWEEK . . . .☐ -6
MacUser . . . .☐ -7
PC Computing . . . .☐ -8
PC Magazine . . . .☐ -9
PC WEEK . . . .☐ -0
Windows Sources . . . .☐ -x
Other (Please specify): _____ ☐ -y

Please turn page.

PLEASE TAPE HERE ONLY—DO NOT STAPLE

6. What is your level of experience with personal computers? With the subject of this book?

	With PCs	With subject of book
Beginner.............	☐ -1 (24)	☐ -1 (25)
Intermediate..........	☐ -2	☐ -2
Advanced.............	☐ -3	☐ -3

7. Which of the following best describes your job title?

Officer (CEO/President/VP/owner)........ ☐ -1 (26)
Director/head........................ ☐ -2
Manager/supervisor.................... ☐ -3
Administration/staff.................... ☐ -4
Teacher/educator/trainer............... ☐ -5
Lawyer/doctor/medical professional....... ☐ -6
Engineer/technician.................... ☐ -7
Consultant.......................... ☐ -8
Not employed/student/retired............ ☐ -9
Other (Please specify): _____ ☐ -0

8. What is your age?

Under 20............................ ☐ -1 (27)
21-29............................... ☐ -2
30-39............................... ☐ -3
40-49............................... ☐ -4
50-59............................... ☐ -5
60 or over.......................... ☐ -6

9. Are you:

Male................................ ☐ -1 (28)
Female.............................. ☐ -2

Thank you for your assistance with this important information! Please write your address below to receive our free catalog.

Name: _____
Address: _____
City/State/Zip: _____

Fold here to mail. 2524-06-07

BUSINESS REPLY MAIL
FIRST CLASS MAIL   PERMIT NO. 1612   OAKLAND, CA

POSTAGE WILL BE PAID BY ADDRESSEE

Ziff-Davis Press
5903 Christie Avenue
Emeryville, CA 94608-1925
Attn: Marketing

ZIFF-DAVIS
ZD
PRESS

NO POSTAGE
NECESSARY
IF MAILED IN
THE UNITED
STATES